An Energy Field More Intense Than War

Syracuse Studies on Peace and Conflict Resolution
Harriet Hyman Alonso, Charles Chatfield, and Louis Kriesberg
Series Editors

An Energy Field More Intense Than War

*The Nonviolent Tradition and
American Literature*

MICHAEL TRUE

Syracuse University Press

First Edition 1995
95 96 97 98 99 00 01   6 5 4 3 2 1

Permission to reprint prose or poetry from the following sources is gratefully acknowledged:

HarperCollins for lines of poetry from Robert Bly, *The Light Around the Body,* New York: Harper and Row, 1967; and from Carolyn Forche, *The Country Between Us,* New York: Harper and Row, 1981.

W. W. Norton for lines of poetry from the forthcoming *Passing Through,* by Stanley Kunitz, in 1995, and from the *Poems of Stanley Kunitz, 1928–1978,* with the permission of W. W. Norton and Company, Inc. Copyright © 1944, 1971, and renewed © 1972 by Stanley Kunitz.

W. W. Norton for prose from *Against Forgetting: Twentieth-Century Poetry of Witness,* edited by Carolyn Forche, New York: W. W. Norton, 1993.

Thunder's Mouth Press for lines of poetry by June Jordan, *Living Room: New Poems.* Copyright © 1985 by June Jordan. Used by permission of the publisher.

Harvard University Press. Reprinted by permission of the publisher of *Play in the Dark: Whiteness and the Literary Imagination* by Toni Morrison, Cambridge, Mass.: Harvard Univ. Press, Copyright © 1992.

Random House for lines of poetry from William Meredith, *Partial Accounts.* Copyright © 1987 by William Meredith. Reprinted by permission of Alfred A. Knopf, Inc.

Ecco Press for lines of poetry from *The Collected Poems, 1931–1987,* by Czeslaw Milosz. Copyright © 1988 by Czeslaw Milosz Royalties, Inc. First published by the Ecco Press in 1988. Reprinted by permission.

University Press of New England for lines of poetry from David Ignatow, "I am dreaming of the funeral of the world," in *New and Collected Poems, 1970–1985.* Copyright © 1986 by David Ignatow, Wesleyan Univ. Press, by permission of Univ. Press of New England.

New Directions for lines of poetry from Denise Levertov, *Breathing the Water.* Copyright © 1987 by Denise Levertov; *Poems, 1960–1967.* Copyright © 1966 by Denise Levertov; *Candles in Babylon.* Copyright © 1982 by Denise Levertov. Reprinted by permission of New Directions Publ. Corp.

Page 170 constitutes a continuation of this copyright page.

Library of Congress Cataloging-in-Publication Data

True, Michael.
    An energy field more intense than war : the nonviolent tradition and American literature / Michael True.—1st ed.
        p. cm.—(Syracuse studies on peace and conflict resolution)
    Includes bibliographical references and index.
    ISBN 0-8156-2679-7 (cl : alk. paper).—ISBN 0-8156-0367-3 (pb : alk. paper)
        1. American literature—History and criticism. 2. Nonviolence in literature. 3. Social justice in literature. 4. Peace movements in literature. 5. Literature and society—United States—History. 6. Politics and literature—United States—History. I. Title. II. Series.
PS169.N65T78   1995
810.9'355—dc20   95-13288

To my students, colleagues, and friends in China

Michael True is a professor of English at Assumption College. He is the author of *Ordinary People: Family Life and Global Values* (1990) and *To Construct Peace* (1991); editor of *Daniel Berrigan: Poetry, Drama, Prose* (1988); and Convenor, Nonviolent Commission, International Peace Research Association.

. . . before we plow an unfamiliar patch
It is well to be informed about the winds,
About the variations in the sky,
The native traits and habits of a place,
What each locale permits, and what denies.

—Virgil

If we are free, we are free to choose a tradition, and we find in the past as well as the present our poets of outrage —like Melville—and our poets of possibility—like Whitman.

—Muriel Rukeyser

For some time now I have been thinking about the validity or vulnerability of a certain set of assumptions conventionally accepted among literary historians and critics and circulated as "knowledge."

—Toni Morrison

Contents

Preface

Since the early European settlements in North America—and particularly in the United States—writers and artists have imagined, even projected, a vision of a society based upon peaceful cooperation and social justice. Their literary works render, dramatize, or reflect upon a concept that social scientists refer to as "positive peace."

These poems, stories, and essays explore concrete ways of resolving conflict, resisting injustice, and building a just social order without harming persons. They recognize, in the words of the poem from which this book takes its title, that peace is not merely the absence of war, but "an energy field more intense than war." The values that they recommend and uphold are reflected in Cesar Chavez's statement that "the truest act of courage, the strongest act of humanity, is to sacrifice ourselves for others in a totally nonviolent struggle for justice."

Although writings in this tradition resemble conventional proclamations recommending peace reform, their tone and attitude tend to be provocative, even disputatious, rather than conciliatory. "Being a pacifist forces you into a strange kind of aggression sometimes," as William Stafford, poet and conscientious objector, once said. Although reconciliation is the goal (end) of nonviolence, writings in the tradition recognize and accept the inevitability of conflict in human affairs—and the need for communal action (means) in resolving it. They assume generally, as Paul Goodman said, that "without confrontation it is impossible to reason, create, solve."

A new and somewhat inadequate term, "nonviolence" is nonetheless the most precise and useful word for naming concepts and strategies associated with initiating social change without violence to persons. It is the nearest English equivalent to Gandhi's Sanscrit word, *satyagraha* (literally, truth force) and certainly more accurate than "passive resistance" or "nonresistance," as nonviolence was called in the nineteenth century.

Staughton Lynd's definition of nonviolence as "the vision of love as an agent for fundamental social change" conveys something of the religious basis of nonviolence in the American tradition. Activists committed to and researchers interested in nonviolence primarily as a strategy, on the other hand, define nonviolence more pragmatically as a method of wielding social, political, and economic power. In the writings discussed in this book, both definitions apply.

Although literary documents in this tradition question conventional thinking that regards war as inevitable or violence as innate to humankind, they are written by men and women of varying political persuasions: pamphlets by William Penn (1644–1718) and Howard Zinn (b. 1921); memoirs—from John Woolman's *Journal* (1774) to Barbara Deming's *Prison Notes* (1966) and David Dellinger's *From Yale to Jail* (1993); novels —from Nathaniel Hawthorne's *The House of the Seven Gables* (1851) to Norman Mailer's *Armies of the Night* (1968); essays—from Adin Ballou's "Non-Resistance: A Basis for Christian Anarchism" (1854) to William James's "The Moral Equivalent of War" (1910) and Martin Luther King's "Letter from Birmingham Jail" (1963); poems—from Karl Shapiro's "Conscientious Objector" (1945) to Reed Whittemore's "Reflections Upon a Recurrent Suggestion by Civil Defense Authorities That I Build a Bombshelter in My Back Yard" (1956) and Denise Levertov's "Making Peace" (1987).

Not surprisingly, some people regard the term "nonviolent tradition," as applied to the United States, as an oxymoron. European settlements and American expansion were often accompanied by annihilating, conquering, or subjugating indigenous peoples; and an aggressive foreign policy perpetuated an attitude that continues to dominate American life and culture. Since the Second World War, a tolerance of violence, amounting at times to a religious faith in it, has shaped this country's foreign and domestic policies. After Hiroshima, "to set an arbitrary moment," killing became "the ordinary civil method of furthering civic ends," Daniel Berrigan has said.

The purpose of this book is not to criticize that dominant ideology or to decry its effects, but to point to a neglected, persistent counterculture reflecting different priorities. At a time when four to ten times as many people per 100,000 die by violence in the United States as in other industrialized nations, cultural artifacts associated with a refusal to kill deserve more attention and reflection than historians and social scientists usually award them.

The primary source for this wide-ranging—but by no means comprehensive—study is written discourse describing or reflecting initiatives for nonviolent social change. Although obviously indebted to recent literary criticism, I have chosen to write a broad survey, rather than a detailed study of individual works, and to leave the task of refining the methodology to other occasions or writers, should they find some merit in it.

This book is about a large subject and a complex relationship: the literature of the United States and its social and political history. It centers on writers who imagined or projected a culture somewhat different from the one that has emerged. Their hopes and efforts are part of a complete story about what is and what might have been—as well as about possible choices for the future. Or so I hope to illustrate in the discussion that follows, beginning with a survey of pamphlets, memoirs, and stories in the first two centuries of the European settlements, then moving to representative poems, stories, and memoirs from the later two centuries of the new nation.

In writing about the relationship between the nonviolent tradition and American literature, I have benefited from the experience and insights of many people. My greatest debt is to those who live the tradition—including men and women I have known through the American Friends Service Committee, the Catholic Worker movement, and the Conference on Peace Research, Education, and Development. I have also been sustained and encouraged by the work of several contemporary poets; haunted by the threat of nuclear war during the cold war years, they not only resisted but also imagined alternatives to the violence of the status quo. As before in our literary history, poets have not failed us in their efforts to tell "the whole truth." In the face of a dominant, often imperial, ideology, they actively resist arguments justifying or tolerating "massive assured destruction"; when few are disposed to listen, these artists envision and present alternative views of a civil society.

In learning about the history of nonviolence, I am indebted to scholars who took an interest in it when much of the academic community was preoccupied with everything else. Among various writings, those of Peter Brock, Charles Chatfield, Staughton Lynd, and the late Charles DeBenedetti are indispensable. I have relied as well on the work and the example of several social scientists, especially Kenneth Boulding and Johan Galtung. Among standard works on American literature, I am indebted to Richard Slotkin's studies of another mythology, "regeneration through violence" on the American frontier, and particularly to Sacvan Bercovitch's studies of culture and ideology from the Puritans to the present. Martin Green's invaluable books on Tolstoy and Gandhi, and about English literary history of the early twentieth century, helped me to understand nonviolence as a response to "empire" in various cultural settings.

Without the encouragement and the example of Gordon C. Zahn, I might not have expanded a bibliographical essay in *War or Peace?: The Search for New Answers,* ed. Thomas Shannon (1980), which preceded this book. I am grateful to the late Ammon Hennacy for his firsthand knowledge of and many contributions to the nonviolent tradition; to Bill Barry for his lively and extensive knowledge of labor history; and to David J. O'Brien for friendship and cooperation on projects related to peace studies. Cynthia Maude-Gembler helped by her enthusiastic support of this project, as did Elizabeth Ann True by her editorial assistance. I owe a special debt to William R. Shannon and Charles Chatfield for thoughtful readings of the manuscript and suggestions for improving it, though neither they, nor others previously acknowledged, are responsible for whatever shortcomings remain.

The Assumption College Faculty Research Committee has been generous in supporting my research and writing, and I am grateful to my colleagues and the administration for this encouragement. Undergraduate students at Assumption, Holy Cross, and Colorado colleges, as well as people, in this country and abroad, who responded to my slide presentation, "The American Tradition of Nonviolence," provided information and insights from their experience and reading.

As before, the encouragement and help of Mary Pat True have been invaluable; she and our six children have lived with my efforts to understand and to write about the relationship between literature and nonviolence for some time. These efforts began, haltingly, during my teaching at an African-American college in North Carolina during the civil rights movement and have continued through campaigns against U.S. wars in Southeast Asia and elsewhere, to the present moment.

Writing this book, I kept remembering the intelligent, resourceful, and courageous young people who initiated and sustained the democratic uprising in China in 1989, perhaps the largest and surely one of the most consequential nonviolent movements in history. It included former students, colleagues, and friends from my time living, teaching, and traveling there over a seven-year period. This book is dedicated to them.

Worcester, Massachusetts   Michael True
January 1995

Reclaiming a Tradition

[Nonviolence] is a state of activity, ever fighting the good fight,
ever foremost to assail unjust power . . . in a world-wide spirit.
It is passive only in this sense—that it will not return evil for
evil.

—William Lloyd Garrison[1]

Violence is so much a part of Ameri-
can culture in the late twentieth century that one is likely to think of it as
the dominant characteristic. People from abroad who know the United
States only through its aggressive foreign policy and its popular culture—
including gangster/counterinsurgency/war films—certainly perceive us as
a violent people. D. H. Lawrence, writing in the 1920s, said that the
"essential American soul is hard, isolate, stoic, and a killer." H. Rap
Brown's argument, in the 1960s, that "violence is as American as apple
pie" is supported by the actual and latent violence inherent in our trillion-
dollar military budget and our role as the major supplier of armaments to
the world. At any moment, forty or so countries—adversaries and allies—
are killing with or dying by weapons "Made in the U.S.A."

There is considerable evidence, nonetheless, that violence is abhorrent
to the culture of the United States. A natural revulsion against war made
it necessary for Woodrow Wilson, for example, to "win" a propaganda
campaign at home in 1917, before waging war abroad. The president
"saved the world for democracy" by sending seventy-five thousand prose-
lytizers across the United States advocating armed intervention, then by
imposing congressional statutes, imprisoning dissenters, suppressing publications, and harassing critics.[2] And still workers and conscientious objectors resisted.

Numerous pamphlets, songs, and books from the seventeenth century to the present suggest that the impulse to resist injustice, to resolve conflict, and to bring about social change while rejecting violence is also "as American as apple pie." Or so a broad literary history indicates to anyone interested in recovering important elements of our buried or "disguised" past, in poetry, fiction, and nonfiction.

Although only occasionally recognized in standard histories of American culture, the literary record of nonviolence is extensive, dramatizing a persistent, occasionally disciplined countercultural search for alternatives to violence. A poem by John Beecher (1904–1989), descendant of the great abolitionist family, is representative. A description of the San Francisco-to-Moscow peace walk as it crossed the Oklahoma prairie in the late winter of 1961, "Engagement at the Salt Fork" conveys a sense of the gentle, persistent strength of the American tradition of nonviolence:

> Like tumbleweeds before the wind we moved
> across the continent's huge heedless face.
> . . . .
> Blasts, born on Yukon tundras, knifed us through
> and buffeted our sign: *Man Will End War or*
> *War Will End Man.* Handful that we were,
> armed men patrolled us, secret agents sped
> ahead to warn the elevator towns. . . . As if we were
> the ghosts of banished Cherokees come back,
> the guilty strip shook in its cowboy boots.[3]

"Handful" that they were—and are—nonviolent activists over three and one-half centuries have evoked a considerable literary response from their contemporaries. And as Beecher suggests, their enduring challenge to violence and injustice evokes memories of earlier Native American resistance to conquest.

The "signs" of the nonviolent tradition are everywhere in the literary history of the United States, including that most elemental and influential text, *Leaves of Grass* (1835). One of Whitman's hopes for that book—and the voice informing it—are relevant here: that "before me all the armies and soldiers of the earth shall yet bow—and all the weapons of war become impotent."[4] With writings by Quaker mystics George Fox and John Woolman in his background, Whitman's poems and essays anticipate the work of later authors, from Jane Addams to Allen Ginsberg, who acknowledge their indebtedness.

Early European settlers, particularly those associated with William

Penn's Holy Experiment, thought about and acted out various ways of living at peace with their neighbors. Even before coming to live in the colonies, they made important decisions about community that influenced the course of literary and social history and shaped the new nation. Often, as with Penn and John Woolman, the quest for peace brought nonviolent activists into close association with Native American cultures. These influences regarding community are evident in artifacts and social movements—including "utopian" communities related to but beyond the scope of this study—from the beginning.

Nonviolent activists offered alternatives—choices, one might say—to accepted, more conventional ways of resisting injustice and resolving conflict. In their efforts to understand and to live these values, they challenged, if somewhat inadvertently, the so-called just-war theory (that is, justifications for making war) associated with Augustine and Thomas Aquinas that has dominated most ethical thinking about war and conflict in Western culture.

Poets, novelists, and social and literary critics of the nineteenth and twentieth centuries have been similarly preoccupied with the implications of nonviolence, in their writing about the struggles of individual abolitionists, feminists, Christian anarchists, conscientious objectors, nuclear resisters—and the communities that sustained them. Exploring concepts associated with nonviolence—pacifism and civil disobedience, as well as love and power—this body of literature includes work by people both sympathetic and unsympathetic to the influence of nonviolence.

In some instances, writers associated with nonviolence are religious pacifists, people for whom "nonresistance" is a way of life; in other instances, they are nonpacifists, people committed to nonviolence as a tactic or interested in it merely as a focal point or theme in fiction and poetry. During the abolitionist and feminist movements of the 1840s and 1850s, for example, William Lloyd Garrison and Adin Ballou were visible, vocal advocates of nonviolent direct action. At the same time, Nathaniel Hawthorne criticized, even satirized, social reformers—both violent and nonviolent—and their effect on (he would say their threat to) civil society. Politically conservative, Hawthorne nonetheless wrote insightful dramatizations, in fiction, of concepts associated with nonviolence, including the theoretical and practical implications of what is now called "conflict resolution."

Different in tone, but related in theme, are literary works dramatizing the contrast between the dream of peace that brought people to the American continent and the culture of violence that they found once they arrived. Long before Allen Ginsberg excoriated America's adoration of

Moloch in *Howl* (1955) or Robert Bly lamented the contrast between Thomas Jefferson's "hope in new oats" and "those being eaten by America" (1967),[5] Thomas Paine argued that the extremes of affluence in the American nation proved that "some extraordinary violence has been committed upon . . . the rugged face of society."[6] Similarly, in the same year that Bly's poem, "Those Being Eaten by America," appeared in an award-winning collection, Martin Luther King, Jr., described his own government as "the greatest purveyor of violence in the world."[7]

Because nonviolence is, at base, a revolutionary challenge to injustice and violence, it has long been associated with other kinds of radical dissent, and its literary record includes writings by social reformers punished or excluded by the established order, church or state. Some early peace activists were antinomian "radicals" or complete "nonresisters"; others associated with troublemakers rather different from themselves—labor agitators, socialists, anarchists—even as they drew the line at killing, no matter what the justification.

A writer's political persuasion—right, left, or center; capitalist, anarchist, or socialist—is often less important, however, than his or her responses to specific issues of nonviolence, just as labels seldom tell us much about an artist's preoccupations in a particular work or at a particular point in his or her life. More relevant in this history are an essayist's manner of addressing injustices in American culture, a novelist's insights into how personal or social conflicts are resolved, or a poet's reflections on how someone negotiates his or her way across a hostile political landscape.

The theme of nonviolence in American literature is obviously related to the theme of violence, as well as to other preoccupations that have characterized written discourse in the United States since the early European settlements. For this reason, it is important, in the midst of occasional confusion, to be as precise as possible about terminology, particularly *violence* and *nonviolence*. Among activists and strategists, the relationship between the two has been cause for considerable discussion, as the words take on new associations and implications. These statements, by Gandhi and Dorothy Day respectively, are representative: "Violence is any day preferable to impotence. There is hope for a violent man to become nonviolent. There is no such hope for the impotent."[8] "Far better to revolt violently than to do nothing about the poor destitute."[9]

The confusion surrounding the word *violence* is the result of considerable change in its denotation and connotation since 1800. As E. J. Hobsbawm said, "Of all the vague words of the late 1960s, violence is very nearly the trendiest and most meaningless." In the midst of what he calls "a general atmosphere of disorientation and hysteria," old confusions perpetuate themselves.[10] When the same word, *violence,* is used to describe both the destruction of property, as in the Boston Tea Party, and the destruction of thousands (potentially millions) of people in a nuclear war, we become aware of the word's limitations in "naming" the concept. As late as 1968, *violence* did not even appear in the *International Encyclopedia of Social Science.* In the apocalyptic rush of contemporary events, we risk destroying ourselves before we have a word to describe what has happened to us, as Hannah Arendt once suggested.

The Latin root (*violencia*) signified vehemence, a passionate and uncontrolled force, the opposite of a calculated exercise of power. Traditionally, it meant "to pervert some object, natural or human, from its 'natural' course of development" and "to exceed some limit or norm." Political theorists of the eighteenth century—Locke, Rousseau, Montesquieu—agreed, generally, that violence could not regenerate people or society and they, unlike later political philosophers, set limits to its "justifiable province."[11] In the American colonies, as well, people used the word without necessarily meaning violence in the modern sense, connoting limitless destruction.[12] Colonists generally regarded *violence* as a last resort, and hoped initially to accomplish political reform by *nonviolent* means.

Since Marx—and perhaps Edmund Burke—*violence* has been extended to include ever widening, particularly calculated, means of destruction. This is quite understandable, given the proliferation of technological weapons over the last two centuries. The change has deprived us of an earlier tradition, nevertheless, which allowed for radical social change (*revolution*) without people resorting inevitably to war and killing.

Our understanding of *nonviolence,* a new word, is similarly frustrated by the word's failure to convey the concept's meaning and purpose. Still omitted from some dictionaries, *nonviolence* is burdened by a negative prefix that causes inevitable confusion for anyone unfamiliar with its history, much as *non-European, non-white,* and *non-Catholic* do in other contexts. New experience evokes, eventually, more precise "naming," as I. A. Richards indicated years ago; in the meantime, activists, strategists, and researchers attempt to clarify basic terms and issues already current.

Gene Sharp, a major theorist and strategist, has said that the trouble with most discussions of *nonviolence* is that they say what you cannot do, rather than what you can do. In a poem about religious pacifists in India, William Meredith suggests that the inadequacy of the English word *nonviolence* relates to a deeper cultural problem. In "The Jain Bird Hospital in Delhi," he describes the Jains' "trust in faith, cognition and non-violence / to release them from rebirth." They "preached the doctrine of *ahimsa,* / which in our belligerent tongue becomes *non-violence.*"[13]

Connotations of nonviolence have emerged, since about 1800, as new strategies and definitions of community associated with original values have presented themselves. Along the way, "nonviolence" went by other names. In the 1840s, although Elihu Burritt and others called it "passive resistance," Burritt spoke of it as a "force," nonetheless, "which any community or country might employ successfully in repelling and disarming despotism; whatever amount of bayonet power it might have at its command."[14]

Although practitioners have regarded nonviolence as active rather than passive, as a positive force rather than as a negative reaction, some historians and political scientists continue to associate nonviolence mistakenly with "inaction," their apparent assumption being that "nothing is being done" until armaments and killing are involved. Peter Maurin, cofounder of *The Catholic Worker* and an admirer of the Wobblies, had a more appropriate sense of the term as a means of righting old wrongs and rebuilding community, or "building a new society in the shell of the old."

The following survey of literary documents indicates that *nonviolence* has a history, just as *force* or *power* or *authority* have. (Attending to that history may help political philosophers and others to avoid common misuses and misunderstandings of the term.) As a literary history, the survey has implications, also, regarding a methodology for understanding and applying nonviolence in the United States—and in other countries. It suggests that how nonviolence works is best understood in relation to the culture that gives it meaning; and that although general principles help to explain nonviolent campaigns whenever and wherever they occur, it is best to see them within the political context that is being addressed. The American effort to resist the war system, as Merle Curti said sixty years ago, has been influenced by American ideals, as well as by historic processes such as "the conquest of the frontier, the coming of the immigrants, internal conflicts . . . the development of technology and an urban society."[15] One might expect campaigns in other countries to be shaped by similar cultural phenomena.

This survey also presents contrasts between the history of peace reform and the history of nonviolence (similar, in some ways, to contrasts between "antiwar" literature and "nonviolence" literature). Attending to those differences enhances our appreciation and understanding of both approaches to social change and of the impulses that inform them.

Peace movements—represented by groups such as the American Peace Society and the Carnegie Institute for International Peace—arose out of a general commitment to moral values opposed to war. Responsible for initiating and sustaining various associations committed to world peace, these reform movements limited themselves, generally, to making recommendations to governments and heads of state, only occasionally resorting to direct action themselves. Ignored by those in power, these associations shied away from direct confrontation or from bold new initiatives in times of crisis. Their leaders were usually unprepared to take serious risks, personal or communal, to further their goals. They regarded "voting for the right"—that is, trusting to the Property Party, as Gore Vidal calls the Democratic/Republican coalition—as "doing something for the right." When push comes to shove—that is, when Congress declares war or the United States bombs or invades another country— "peace reform movements" falter or collapse. "Between wars," as Ammon Hennacy used to say, "everybody is for peace."

"Nonviolent movements," on the other hand, have been inherently "pro-active." They depend upon individual initiative, symbolized by the man who responded to the 1963 Cuban missile crisis by carrying a sign saying "NO!" into the town square. Nonviolent movements usually begin as responses to particular injustices. Like "violent" movements for social change, they introduce a new factor into the power equation, even when public opinion and policy are heavily weighted against them. The early abolitionists and the activists against the war in Vietnam in 1965, for example, faced overwhelming opposition. In the latter case, less than 25 percent of the voters opposed the war, and anyone who advocated ending the draft (central to national policy from about 1940 on) was regarded as a romantic or a fool. Then, unexpectedly, in 1973, inductions ended, as a result of nonviolent resistance at various levels. Similarly, "the Brotherhood Movement," initiated in the early 1940s, required disciplined resistance to the status quo, where thousands of people risked beatings, imprisonment, and death, before it achieved victory for Civil Rights in the 1960s.

Although they may employ conventional efforts for change, such as petitions and legislative lobbying, nonviolent activists assume direct responsibility for change. They challenge the legitimacy of those in authority and sometimes threaten their power base; their purpose, as Gandhi often said, is to provoke a response. The Wobblies, the Socialist Party, and the Non-Conscription League disobeyed the draft law, for example, after it was initiated in 1917, and suffered harassment, jail, and exile for doing so. During the Vietnam War, members of RESIST publicly advocated outright rejection of "illegitimate authority," as the government tried unsuccessfully, through various conspiracy trials, to discredit, then to crush, the antiwar movement.

Philosophically, nonviolence owes much more to the seventeenth than to the nineteenth century—to Hobbes, Milton, and Locke, rather than Rousseau, Shelley, or Marx. It is more closely associated with those crying "No taxation without representation" than with those calling for "Liberty, Equality, Fraternity." Although the terms may be general (and potentially misleading), nonviolence is primarily practical and strategic, rather than romantic or utopian. In attempting to make ends and means compatible with each other, as Mulford Sibley said of the pacifist, the nonviolent activist "is both a revolutionary and a political realist,"[16] while remaining skeptical about any revolution that advocates "killing the killers in order to stop the killing."[17]

The Quaker and Mennonite responses to war and violence in the seventeenth century, though tentative and exploratory, were thoughtful, political (one might even say tactical) decisions, maintained in the face of opposition; they were not impulsive gestures to "bring on the revolution." Nonviolence in the seventeenth century, as with Hobbes's Leviathan image for the State, coincided with the effort to bring an end to religious strife, as Christians randomly killed one another in the name of Christ.

Although the eighteenth-century essays of Paine and Jefferson about "rights" inform the nonviolent tradition, it is not defined primarily by that discussion. A direct challenge to hierarchical structures, the tradition is at the same time an attempt to enhance and to further the democratic process. And although Marx's insights about economic structures and moral values in the nineteenth century have obviously influenced nonviolence, as well as other political strategies, his preoccupations do not explain its basic methods and goals.

Pauline Maier, writing about Samuel Adams and his allies of the late eighteenth century, argued that "successful revolutionary leaders are not violent and irresponsible anarchists, but politic persons of intense discipline for whom the public cause purges mundane considerations of self."[18] Among nonviolent strategists, Adams's contemporary, John Woolman, was perhaps the first to indicate the relationship between self-denial and the transforming power of nonviolence. And in the writings of Tolstoy, Gandhi, and King, that concept occasionally informs discussions about when to push forward, when to negotiate, when to retreat, and when to forgive. Throughout history, nonviolent activists have been willing to sacrifice themselves or even to die rather than to harm or to kill human beings, however just the cause.

Because of these qualities and characteristics, nonviolent activists have much in common with what Gordon S. Wood and other historians regard as "radical" or "revolutionary" about the formative period before and during the American struggle for independence.[19] The ending of British rule, the Quaker physician Benjamin Rush once said, was only the first act in a great drama; although it did not play itself out as he and others hoped or expected, subsequent acts of the drama, as the literature suggests, retain elements of that earlier vision. During periods of social change, nonviolent activists resort to new and ingenious forms of political action, in a "continuing cycle of political renewal."[20] The result is a transformation in people's relationships to one another—among colonists in the late eighteenth century or among Southerners in the mid-twentieth century. At other times, especially amid preparations for war and the ambitions of empire, the vision of a peaceable kingdom and the strategies for achieving it are lost or forgotten.

The literary survey that follows begins with early essays and pamphlets, then moves forward in time, with each chapter discussing selected works that reflect the nonviolent tradition at that point. The focus is on documents with aesthetic as well as historical claims on the reader's attention, although "literature" in this case refers to "written discourse," not just to "belles lettres," in the traditional sense. Subject matter is a central reason for including a particular document; but a writer's success in combining subject and style, argument and artistry, is an important consideration as well.

The fact that the relationship between nonviolence and literature has been largely ignored is a disservice not only to extensive writings that reflect the influence of nonviolence but also to cultural institutions that it informs. Two generations ago, the American historian J. Franklin Jameson argued that all the varied activities of people in the same country "have intimate relations with each other, and . . . one cannot obtain a satisfactory view of any one of them by considering it apart from the others."[21] In an effort to reclaim a tradition, I have tried, without overstating the case, to suggest its place in the larger cultural setting.

Nonviolence is obviously "a"—not "the"—tradition in American letters, one layer in a multilayered archeological dig, one voice in a chorus, one of several trails into the new world. Only periodically aware of itself, it is sometimes halting and contradictory in its development. Although the path is wiggly and overgrown, it is nonetheless significantly there, distinctive. Regarding it as such enables one to understand how, at various points in history, it veered, went astray, or practically disappeared, then reemerged and moved confidently in several directions.

An Energy Field More Intense Than War

1

The Peaceable Kingdom
1607–1776

> The peaceable profession which we have long made to the world (which constitutes a very amiable part of our religious character) will not admit of our taking up arms.
>
> —Timothy Davis, 1776[1]

In the century and a half between the landings in Virginia and Massachusetts and the American Revolution, European settlers contributed to the history of nonviolence directly and indirectly, in various ways. In Puritan New England, they disobeyed discriminatory laws against religious dissenters. In Pennsylvania and Maryland, Quakers and others refused to participate in or pay for violence against Native Americans, even as others justified a resort to arms. In slaveholding regions, colonists "broke the law" by teaching African Americans to read and to write. And during the Revolutionary War, pacifists refused to justify killing, even as they resisted British rule.

In this period, as later, people with little or no knowledge of "strategy," that is, organized resistance, contributed to the tradition by individual acts of courage that led ultimately to significant social change. Anne Hutchinson (1591–1643), antinomian preacher, and Roger Williams (1603–1683), separatist and "leveler," contributed to a tradition of conscientious dissent by standing firm against laws later regarded as unjust and suffering the consequences. Eventually, both were brought to trial, were banished from their home territory of Massachusetts, and took up residence in Rhode Island.

Like the early Quakers in England and the colonies, Williams and

Hutchinson were ostracized for remaining true to principle—in Williams's case, as he said, because Christ demanded it. Although their cases are quite different from one another, as well as from the cases of others who endured similar fates, their nonviolent direct action helped to further religious tolerance in the colonies—and by extension, the new nation.

Quakers reaching Massachusetts in 1656 were confined to ships in the harbor, under oppressive conditions. Finally allowed to land, many were put on trial, were whipped and banished. On October 27, 1659, William Robinson and Marmaduke Stevenson were hanged; and the following June, Mary Dyer, whose statue overlooks Boston Common from the grounds of the Massachusetts State House, was exiled, then killed because she refused to absent herself permanently from the colony. (Eventually, under order of Charles II, Quakers who had been condemned or imprisoned by the court were returned to England.)

During the same period, people in other colonies suffered persecution and contributed to religious liberty for beliefs and practices resembling those of Hutchinson and Williams. Insisting on rights of conscience, including exemption from military service for their children, Quakers and Mennonites in Pennsylvania and Maryland endured terrible hardships for their refusal to take up arms or to pay taxes for war.

These "troublemakers," the civil disobedients of their day, confronted laws and conventions much in the manner of those who argued against slavery or the draft later on. As with militant abolitionists, labor agitators, feminists, and war resisters, Quakers of the colonial period were regarded with disdain by their contemporaries and sometimes by writers and historians, who only slowly recognized their contributions to democratic principle and the common good.

Nathaniel Hawthorne (1804–1864), for example—though fascinated by them and drawn to them as background figures in his stories and novels —cast a cold eye on Quaker "extravagances." In a prefatory note to "The Gentle Boy" (1832), he says "the government of Massachusetts Bay indulged two members of the Quaker sect with the crown of martyrdom" because of their militancy. Here and elsewhere, Hawthorne implies that seventeenth-century Quakers were "asking for it" and even deserved what they got.

Other early European settlers courted trouble or "broke the law" —closely identified with religious practice—by consorting with Native Americans. Roger Williams, among other religious nonconformists, criticized the royal charter for condemning Native American rights. Thomas Morton (1590?–1647), an Anglican trader and writer later satirized in Hawthorne's "Maypole of Merry Mount," posed a threat to Puritan society in his dealings with Native Americans, for rather different reasons.

And more than one historian has regarded the Puritan hallmark and the faith that undergirded it as "a volatile mixture" of self-assurance as God's saviors of Christianity, and fear of their enemies, "Indians, Quakers, Catholics, and the backsliders in their own midst."[2] Thus did *dissent* and *nonviolence* come to be associated with one another, as various groups began to challenge the established order during the period of the early European settlements.

Although often lumped together because of their pacifism, members of traditional peace churches—Quakers, Mennonites, Church of the Brethren, Dunkers, Shakers, Amana Society, and Christadelphians—had varying religious histories and countries of origin. The Quakers—radical Puritans—were primarily English, with links to the Anglican Church, while Mennonites, Brethren, and the others were usually Dutch, German, or Swiss, with Calvinist and Lutheran backgrounds.

As with other emigrants over the centuries, many came to the American colonies to escape persecution in their native lands and to establish communities in keeping with their religious values. Some, less motivated by pacifist beliefs or their objections to violence, found "saving their skins" reason enough to escape conscription and wars in Europe. Whatever the cause, some who had suffered severely in the old world would continue to suffer in the new world.

Following the example of their founder George Fox, who "lived in the virtue of that life and power that took away the occasion of all wars," Quakers in New England faced indignities that they had expected to escape upon leaving England: imprisonment, fines, and exile. In Pennsylvania, an initial cause of persecution was their refusal to take part in the French and Indian Wars. At the same time, some congregations disowned or excluded members who cooperated with military authorities or with practices related to war.

The fact that Pennsylvania—and Maryland, to a lesser degree—was more hospitable to religious dissenters than other colonies accounted for the concentration of "radical" Puritans, Mennonites, and other Anabaptists in those two colonies. One of the first protests against slavery occurred in 1688, when the Mennonite community in Germantown, Pennsylvania, challenged Quakers to free their slaves by asking how anyone opposed to violence could do otherwise. "Yea, rather is it worse for them, which say they are Christians," they argued. "In Europe there are many oppressed for conscience sake; and here there are those oppressed who are of a black color. This make an ill report in all those countries of Europe when people hear that Quakers in the colonies handle men as Quakers in Europe handle their cattle."[3]

Not surprisingly, because pacifists numbered in the tens of thousands there, Pennsylvania was the first region to abolish slavery. Although each of the peace churches contributed acts and policies associated with nonviolence, Quakers provided the most significant body of literature associated with nonviolence during the early European settlements and up to the founding of the new nation.

Among figures whose writings remain significant, William Penn (1644–1718), John Woolman (1720–1772), his associate Anthony Benezet (1713–1784), and Thomas Paine (1737–1809) claim a special place in the history of nonviolence, though for quite different reasons. William Penn—a sophisticated politician and vigorous pamphleteer, a friend to king, Native American, and Quaker brethren alike—is rightfully regarded as the most significant apostle of nonviolence in the seventeenth century. An activist and cultural hero, he helped create a language for peacemaking by writing as well as "doing." To the goals of religious toleration and constitutional government in the colonies he added another: the establishment of a state, "a Quaker Eden almost," governed by the peace principles of the Sermon on the Mount. Rather like the Puritans in Massachusetts building " a city on a hill," the Quakers on the banks of the Delaware River envisioned a Holy Experiment set down in this "new" and unexplored continent.

Because both their political philosophies were shaped by their experience with Anglicanism and both contributed to the extension of religious liberty in the colonies, Roger Williams and William Penn have more in common, perhaps, than their very different attitudes toward the world might suggest—Williams as an intellectual, Penn as a politician. For different reasons, both discouraged English settlers from going to war with the Indians, Williams by recognizing their claims to their homeland and Penn by providing means for resolving conflicts among settlers and Native Americans.

Although the charter for Pennsylvania said that Penn's "charge and office," as a captain-general, enabled him to make war and to pursue enemies and "by God's assistance" to vanquish and to capture them, he relegated such authority to others. His Holy Experiment eventually ended, according to him, because "Quaker deputies . . . found it difficult to deal with the exigencies of government." Others say that "the elevation of what was personal, almost vocational pacifism into a political policy was fraught with danger" from the beginning.[4]

As an experiment, however, early Pennsylvania provided a model and some useful lessons for later attempts at "building the beloved community," including utopian or intentional communities that evolved over the next two centuries. And one can trace a direct line from Penn's arguments regarding the relationship between nonviolence and community in pamphlets written in the 1790s to Jim Corbett's arguments in "Going Up to Zion: The Extension of the Sanctuary Covenant," written in the 1980s.

For anyone interested in the relationship between nonviolent theory and strategy, Penn remains a fascinating figure. As a Quaker, he eventually found it impossible to wear a sword. At the same time, he continued to try to establish guidelines and political policies that were faithful to his own ethical stand, yet "realistic" toward the non-Quaker world. Particularly impressive, in light of later developments in nonviolent strategy in international relations, is his famous *Essay Towards the Present and Future Peace of Europe* (1693), advocating economic sanctions against those who refused to accept arbitration.

William Penn's life and writings retain a value for later generations of nonviolent strategists because of his "divided allegiance" to God and king and his manner of juggling or negotiating those priorities. What some might criticize as a flaw in philosophy others rightly value as a virtue in strategy. Having suffered jail for his religious beliefs, Penn retained an openness to those who ridiculed and persecuted him. In the complicated balancing act of domestic politics, his friendship with the king resulted in his winning special favors for Quakers in England and in the colonies. His ability to focus on specific issues and to think through the implications of his commitment to pacifism attests to his practical genius, if not his philosophical consistency.

Through all these negotiations, Penn retained a positive—one might say characteristically English—attitude toward civil government, an attitude that later nonviolent activists, including early abolitionists and Christian anarchists, abandoned in the heat of the struggle. "Government seems to me a part of religion itself, a thing sacred in its institutions and end," Penn wrote in 1682[5]—an attitude that strategists such as Ballou and Tolstoy rejected. Later activists, including Gandhi and King, agreed with Penn, though with reservations.

Throughout, Penn advocated and practiced nonviolence in his relations with everyone, from English nobility to Native Americans. Reading his pamphlets, one is reminded of Gandhi and King's admonitions to maintain a tolerance for all religious beliefs and practices and (plainly) to "love your enemies." Religious rivalries in sixteenth- and seventeenth-century England, like nuclear ecological concerns in the twentieth century, dramatized the need for tolerance, and Penn stands as one of the principal "contractors," if not architects, of English laws protecting the rights of minorities. His legacy to the new nation strongly resembled his legacy to England, as Quakers took the initiative in pressing for minority rights, including protection under the law for tax resisters, conscientious objectors, and other libertarians advocating humane, though unpopular, reforms.

Although radically different from Penn in background, temperament, and attitude, John Woolman is equally central to the nonviolent tradition. (A young activist of the Vietnam period, for example, called him "the first draft counselor.") By personal example, Woolman—with many "unknown" Quakers of the eighteenth century—dramatized the practicality of Penn's theories and tactics in everyday life, and his *Journal* (1774) may be the most important literary text in this history.

Woolman traveled widely in the colonies, visiting his coreligionists and challenging them to live a nonviolent ethic, and he was admired by Quakers and non-Quakers alike. He wrote a classic treatise almost without intending to:

> Love was the first motion, and then a concern arose to spend some time with the Indians, that I might feel and understand their life and the spirit they live in, if haply I might receive some instruction from them, or they be in any degree helped forward by my following the leadings of Truth amongst them.[6]

This entry, written during the early 1760s, is characteristic in both language and tone.

Although Woolman was interested in social philosophy, he came to his nonviolence through an intense personal faith, weighing each of his public acts against the good of the community. Never defiant or confrontational—or "contentious," as Dorothy Day would say later of Ammon Hennacy and other militants—Woolman took seriously whatever responsibility fell to him as a lawful citizen, as the opening of his reflection on tax resistance suggests: "To refuse the active payment of a tax which our Society generally paid was exceeding disagreeable, but to do a thing contrary to my conscience appeared yet more dreadful."[7]

Recognized as one of the great religious autobiographies, Woolman's *Journal* has a kind of sweetness about it, as several admirers have said, which contributes to its accessibility and power. Emerson praised its wisdom, Charles Lamb its readability, Samuel Taylor Coleridge its hopefulness, George Trevelyan its practicality. American writers as different as John Greenleaf Whittier, the nineteenth-century romantic poet, and Theodore Dreiser, the twentieth-century naturalistic novelist, have acknowledged the journal's influence; others place it beside Thoreau's *Walden* (1854) as an elemental document of the inner life.

Woolman was among the first apostles of nonviolence to distinguish between an antiwar ethic and a positive peace ethic in a practical way. He was not, in other words, merely a so-called dissenter or refuser, who argued against taking up arms to combat Native Americans or "enemies"; Woolman took positive initiatives to live peacefully among them. Personal witnessing, such as refusing to go to war, was not enough; one must also "remove the causes of war that lay concealed in the economic system"— in the slavery system, in the injustices toward Native Americans, and in low wages paid to English postboys.[8] Most important for nonviolence, he left a record of his "experiments with truth," in a memoir that has encouraged others to search out "the way of peace" throughout the world. He was prophetic in linking oppression of "others" nearby with war against "others" far away—an insight associated with abolitionists a century later, and central presently to all nonviolent campaigns.

In his personal life, Woolman helped people to understand the effectiveness of a boycott, a nonviolent tactic that activists and theorists have exploited with considerable success ever since. (Gandhi's burning of cloth, as a protest against the economic conditions among workers, in the early years after he returned to India, is a dramatic example.) In Woolman's case, he quit wearing dyed clothes because dyes were harmful to workers, and gave up using sugar because of the conditions among those who harvested it.

Other contributions to nonviolence strategy included his showing Quakers a way to release their slaves from bondage and to live in harmony with Native Americans, in "Friendly Association for Gaining and Preserving Peace with Indians by Pacific Means"; and although Woolman emphasized the connection between injustice and violence in many of his writings, *A Plea for the Poor* (1763), addressed to fellow Quakers and published posthumously as "A Remembrance and Caution to the Rich" (1793), argues the case with particular skill.

Benjamin Rush's description of Woolman's contemporary and associate, Anthony Benezet, suggests the major concerns of another Quaker pamphleteer of that period: "In one hand [Benezet] carried a subscription paper and a petition; in the other he carried a small pamphlet on the unlawfulness of the African slave-trade directed to the King of Prussia upon the unlawfulness of war" because he insisted that the source of the two evils was the same.[9] Founder of schools for girls and for African Americans and author of "A Caution and Warning to Great Britain and Her Colonies, etc." (1767) against slavery and *The Plainness and Innocent Simplicity of the Christian Religion with Its Salutary Effects, Compared to the Corrupting Nature and Dreadful Effects of War* (1782), Benezet refused to pay taxes to support the French and Indian Wars, as well as the American War of Independence.

Writing to John Jay, president of the Continental Congress in 1779, Benezet, under Woolman's influence, endeavored to remove "any offence which Friends' refusal to take part in matters of a military nature may have raised in thy mind." He was anxious that Congress "distinguish between such who are active in opposition, and those restrained from taking up arms out of a duty to our common beneficent Father who has the hearts of all men in his power."[10] Thus began a conversation between members of peace churches and the government, which led a century and a half later to lawful alternatives to military service under a conscientious objector classification.

In providing relief services for victims on both sides during the Revolutionary War, Quakers anticipated the later work of the American Friends Service Committee (AFSC) and similar committees among the Mennonites and Brethren. Refusing to bear arms against the British, even when they supported the cause of independence, they continued to be regarded with suspicion, nonetheless, because of "fears that British spies lay concealed beneath the Quaker drab."[11] Many of them lost property and furnishings, which were seized without justification, and they endured heavy fines for refusing to kill.

Even for militant rebels, war was a last resort, after they failed to achieve their goal nonviolently. Previously, for example, the North Carolina Regulation and the Boston crowds in the late 1760s employed various methods of nonviolent protest in seeking independence from England: law suits, civil disobedience, petitions, election campaigns, limited destruction of property. "Again and again, the Boston crowd had considered its interest, determined its enemies, and moved in a coordinated and discriminating way to gain its ends through street action."[12] People of higher social status frequently supported and shielded the crowd's leaders when authorities threatened them with punishment or jail.

Activists and agitators developed, with growing sophistication, ordered and organized means of nonviolent social change. Even writers and activists who upheld the people's right of revolution "sought to limit and even deter violence by a series of preconditions that were ever more carefully defined," Pauline Maier has said. This historically significant approach to social change indicated that colonial leaders, "like many modern-day 'revolutionaries,' quickly learned that unrestrained popular violence was counter-productive."[13]

Before embarking on a path of violence, the Sons and Daughters of Liberty sought to expose the violence of the other side through skillful manipulations of public opinion. In the "Boston Massacre," for example, resisters turned public opinion against the British, with the help of Paul Revere's dramatic poster and in various articles in the popular press, including Isaiah Thomas's accounts of the battles of Lexington and Concord in *The Massachusetts Spy*. A reliance upon newspapers, broadsides, and other popular art forms to "get the word out" has remained an important strategy employed by apostles of nonviolence ever since, from Tolstoy's public letters and pamphlets against the imperial army in Russia to Gandhi's popular articles against British rule and reports on his campaign (he wrote an average of 500 words per day, for publication); from King's speeches and pamphlets from jail during the Civil Rights movement to the latest issue of *The Catholic Radical* or *Southern Exposure* or *Peacework*. Advocates of nonviolence built on this "literary" tradition, in labor and antiwar movements, by writing words to old Gospel hymns that they sang on the picket line and in jail.

Other contributions to the rhetoric and style of literature in the nonviolent tradition are associated with the writings and example of Thomas Paine (journalist, versifier, and pamphleteer) and to a lesser degree with those of Thomas Jefferson. Arriving in the colonies in 1774, at the invitation of Benjamin Franklin, and sick abed, Paine had to be carried from the ship and nursed to health during his first weeks in Philadelphia.

In light of his previous experience in supporting workers in England, Paine took the side of the colonists immediately, as if he had assimilated the American ethos upon arrival. Initially, he attacked Parliament's unjust treatment of them, as rightful inheritors of British liberties. In his *Pennsylvania Magazine,* he supported people's struggles for independence around the world, and published a pioneering and blistering attack on slavery, one of several reasons, perhaps, that Pennsylvania was among the first states to free slaves, as the Revolutionary War began.

Paine's popular essays—his *Common Sense* was the country's first bestseller—showed a deep trust in the democratic process, where individual merit, not social position or inherited wealth, established the limit of a person's achievement. Paine, generally sympathetic to nonviolence because of his Quaker background, trusted that people could bring about a just society on their own by applying reason to all areas of life, philosophical as well as practical. He viewed the struggle for individual liberty from an internationalist perspective, as "a citizen of the world," and regarded the American movement for independence as "the cause of all mankind."

Paine's feeling of responsibility for the welfare of all people, regardless of nation, race, sex, or class, is his principal gift to nonviolence. Almost half a century after Paine took as his motto "My country is the world; to do good is my religion," William Lloyd Garrison rephrased it, initially without knowing he was doing so, in his equally famous motto: "My country is the world; my countrymen are all mankind." Later, realizing the Paine association, Garrison used the statement on the masthead of *The Liberator.* In three stanzas of verse for the *Emancipator* (November 1837), he refined the sentiment a bit, ending,

> In every land, in every tribe I see,
> Each bears the image of a gracious God;
> Jews, Greeks, Barbarians, Scythians, bond or free . . .
> And if I roam from east to west, I find.
> "My Country is the world; my countrymen mankind."[14]

Later American writers, improving the language and form, have returned to Paine and Garrison's peculiarly American theme.

Common Sense, published in January 1776, only a year or so after Paine came to the colonies—with 150,000 copies circulating among three million people—succeeded in uniting the multifarious and confused forces among the warring colonies and in resolving conflicts among them. It managed to appeal to Quakers and Germans in one region, to the self-interest of farmers and merchants in another, to radicals and artisans in this region, to conservative merchants and landowners in that. It repeated arguments contained in hundreds of pamphlets previously circulated in the colonies, but with extraordinary clarity, economy, and vigor. Jefferson, in turn, repeated them in more elegant form in the Declaration of Independence, six months later. Both documents have served as models and inspiration for manifestos advocating nonviolent direct action ever since.

In an effort to encourage the Continental Army, particularly in Pennsylvania, Paine wrote the *Crisis* papers, his most belligerent writings, attacking American Tories, Quakers who refused to bear arms, and others who endeavored to negotiate an early peace with Britain. By 1787, even before the Constitution was adopted, Paine, the controversialist, frustrated and shocked by the increasing conservatism of the new nation, left for Paris.

In France, Paine's pamphlets espoused principles that would distinguish his generally nonviolent programs for democratic reforms. His *Prospects on the Rubicon* (1787), for example, includes an eloquent plea against war and "the unforeseen and unsupposed circumstances that war provokes," in a manner resembling Randolph Bourne's discussion of war and herd psychology during World War I. In spite of the fact that "the calamities of war and the miseries it inflicts upon the human species, [and] the thousands and tens of thousands of every age and sex who are rendered wretched by the event," the populace often greets rumors of war enthusiastically, Paine said. Sounding much like critics exposing the Hearst papers for warmongering in the late nineteenth century or Paul Goodman and Gore Vidal ridiculing Pentagon lobbyists for cold-warring in the late twentieth century, Paine condemned those owners and rulers who profited from war in the late eighteenth century: "It is their harvest; and the clamor which these people keep up in newspapers and conversations passes unsuspiciously for the voices of the people."[15]

As one of only two foreign members of the French Assembly, Paine consistently argued for the de-escalation of violence in France as well. Even before leaving England on the way across the channel, he said, "If the French kill their king, it will be a signal for my departure, for I will not abide among sanguinary men," and his courageous speech favoring exile, rather than execution of Louis XVI, almost cost Paine his head.[16] Throughout, his arguments supporting a French constitution, during a long debate over structures for the revolutionary government, indicated an abhorrence of war and killing. That sentiment also informed his later, famous treatises, *The Rights of Man* (1791–92) and *The Age of Reason, Being an Investigation of Truth and of Fabulous Theology* (1794–95), and another great, though much less widely read work, *Agrarian Justice* (1796), published in France before Paine returned to the United States in 1802.

Insistent, unrelenting, in his call for democratic reform, Paine nonetheless understood basic truths about the psychology of social change, including the necessity of giving people time to adapt to it:

> There never yet was any truth or any principle irresistibly obvious that all men believe it at once. Time and reason must cooperate with each other to the final establishment of any principle and therefore those who may happen to be first convinced have not a right to persecute others on whom conviction operates more slowly. The moral principal of revolutions is to instruct, not to destroy. . . . Had a constitution been established two years ago (as ought to have been done) the violences that have since desolated France and injured the character of the Revolution would have been prevented.[17]

When Paine had voted against the execution of Louis XVI, the radical Marat spitefully pointed out that Paine did so because all Quakers opposed capital punishment. And it was true that the French Revolution took a direction different from the one Paine advocated. Eventually, following the rhetorical triumph of Edmund Burke's *Reflections on the Revolution in France* (1790), England declared an ideological war against Paine, as well as friends and allies in his native country, whom it imprisoned or arrested for circulating his *Rights of Man*.

Paine's motto, "My country is the world; to do good is my religion," remains, nonetheless, one of the principal affirmations of the nonviolent tradition. As a "citizen of the world," he committed himself, as did William Lloyd Garrison and later advocates of nonviolence, to "doing justice, loving mercy, and endeavoring to make our fellow creatures happy," as Paine wrote in the preface to *The Age of Reason*.

He took his responsibilities to citizens of England and France (and by extension, to other countries) as seriously as he did his responsibilities to the citizens of his adopted colonies and nation. Espousing and practicing such principled behavior inevitably got Paine into trouble wherever he lived; even after his death, scurrilous and unfounded attacks upon his character continued. A characteristic slander, harsher but only slightly less pointed than others, is that of his biographer, William Cobbett: "Men will learn to express all that is base, malignant, treacherous, unnatural, and blasphemous by one single monosyllable—Paine."

Not surprisingly, anyone hostile to Paine's ideas repeated or initiated these attacks well into this century. Theodore Roosevelt, for example, who called Jane Addams "the most dangerous woman in America," also referred to Paine as a "filthy little atheist." Like others who attack anyone attempting to purge institutional religion of superstition and artifice, Roosevelt either intentionally misrepresented or simply ignored Paine's fascination for and persistent interest in all things religious. One century later, Paine's "historical criticism" of the Bible would become commonplace among Christian theologians.

The best defense of Paine, listing his projects and delineating his values, is perhaps his own, in response to a royal proclamation suppressing *The Rights of Man:*

> If, to expose the fraud and imposition of monarchy, and every species of hereditary government—to lessen the oppression of taxes—to propose plans for the education of helpless infancy, and the comfortable support of the aged and distressed—to endeavor to conciliate nations to each other—to extirpate the horrid practise of war—to promote universal peace, and civilization, and the commerce—and to break the chains of political superstition, and raise degraded man to his proper rank—if these things be libellous, let me live the life of a Libeller, and let the name of LIBELLER be engraved on my tomb.

This statement serves as a kind of catalog of causes embraced by nonviolent activists in the United States ever since.

Paine's last major pamphlet, *Agrarian Justice*, addressed to the political elite rather than to the "ordinary people" he usually spoke for, also belongs to this literary tradition. Its emphasis upon the relationship between peace and justice has since served as the focal point for manifestos for social change as well:

> The rugged face of society, checkered with the extremes of affluence and want, proves that some extraordinary violence has been committed upon it, and calls on justice for redress. . . . It is not charity but a right, not bounty but justice, that I am pleading for. . . . The contrast of affluence and wretchedness continually meeting and offending the eye, is like dead and living bodies chained together.[18]

Describing the consequences of the industrial revolution in his own time, Paine sounds very much like recent commentators describing the exploitation of workers by multinational corporations in underdeveloped and third world countries two centuries later.

The tone and argument of Paine's pamphlets would dominate writings in the nonviolent tradition for some time. His style, stately and vigorous, relied on the radical Puritan tradition associated with Milton's pamphlets of the mid-seventeenth century; on the prophetic and dissenting tradition of the Quakers—militant nonconformists, who risked imprisonment and death for conscience's sake, of the late seventeenth century; and on an emerging "working class"—people on the fringes of society, unsuccessful by conventional standards, dispossessed, with whom Paine had been associated since the mid-eighteenth century. Like Moll Flanders or the figures in Hogarth's engravings on city life, these "ne'er-do-wells" were the "other" England or America, usually excluded from political and religious debate.

The development of his literary style, as seen in an early petition he wrote before leaving for America in 1774, indicates Paine's increasing skill in directing his arguments for justice to an audience of "the plain people from whom he had sprung," as his biographer, David Freeman Hawke, has said. Making the most of an intellectual and political tradition evident in pamphlets circulating in the colonies before his arrival, *Common Sense* speeded up the process of revolution and led directly to the Declaration of Independence. No wonder Edmund Burke and others feared Paine's influence, as later people devoted to the status quo feared Eugene Victor Debs, Emma Goldman, Malcolm X, and Martin Luther King.

Jefferson—rationalist, yet religious in the eighteenth-century manner —shared privately Paine's views on Christianity, and Jefferson's "wee little book," *The Life and Morals of Jesus of Nazareth,* "the authentic accounts and sayings of Jesus," is very much in the spirit of Paine.[19] Like him, Jefferson tended to rely on the conscience of "ordinary people" in political matters as he did in religious matters. No radical he, Jefferson nonetheless shared with many of his contemporaries the democratic leveling that was part of the move toward independence. As far as the history of nonviolence is concerned, this general attitude may have been more decisive in the writings of Paine and Jefferson than the emphasis upon "natural rights." Or so recent historical debate over the Declaration of Independence suggests.

Although the colonists eventually resorted to war in throwing off British rule, the Declaration of Independence retained a spirit of revolution more characteristic of earlier political discourse; its emphasis centered upon principled resistance rather than violent rebellion, in the manner of later revolutionary documents. Somewhat in the same vein, as several historians have noted, the colonists' rallying cry, "No taxation without representation," was inherently conservative, in contrast to the more generalized and abstract *crie de cour,* "Liberty, Equality, Fraternity."

However much the new nation and Jefferson strayed from the ideals and principles associated with the Declaration—including its author's seizure of the Louisiana Territory—the document of July 4, 1776, remains a major reference point for social movements in this country. The Seneca Falls Declaration of Sentiments in 1848, coauthored by Lucretia Mott, abolitionist and nonviolent activist, echoes, even parodies, Jefferson's prose. The Seneca Falls document argues "that all men and women are created equal" and lists "injuries and usurpations on the part of man toward woman," in the manner of Jefferson, with powerful effect.

Among documents central to the nonviolent tradition, the Declaration of Independence, in other words, occupies a very special place, beside Thoreau's "Civil Disobedience" and Martin Luther King's "Letter from Birmingham Jail." In each case, the author's sense of audience, the concreteness of the language, and the particularity of grievances are distinguishing marks. All three "speak" in the right tone of voice, successfully teaching and adapting traditional values regarding the issues of the moment. As Carl Becker said of the Declaration of Independence, the style is candid, simple, striking, yet at the same time urbane, felicitous, haunting. These qualities, more than any set of ideas perhaps, make a knowledge of the Declaration indispensable to any understanding of the nonviolent tradition in this country.

At least three of its central propositions appear over and over again in calls to nonviolent direct action: that governments are organized and sustained for the benefit of the living; that citizens have not only the right but also the duty to overthrow tyrannical governments and—before that —to break oppressive laws; and that citizens owe their allegiance not to one nation but to the whole human family. Staughton Lynd has called the preamble to the Declaration of Independence "the single most concentrated expression of the revolutionary intellectual tradition";[20] it might be designated more accurately as a concentrated expression of the nonviolent tradition.

In the early years of the new nation, Jefferson remained sufficiently "radical" to support Shays's Rebellion of 1786. He wrote from France encouraging the Revolutionary veterans, now farmers in central and western Massachusetts, who rose up against the military-industrial complex in Boston. For that statement on behalf of the farmers and his authorship of the Declaration ten years earlier, Jefferson has won "the hearts and minds" of nonviolent activists ever since. Even Ammon Hennacy (1892–1970), that most demanding of Christian anarchists, gave Jefferson an honored place beside Paine and William Lloyd Garrison among the eighteen men and women in *One Man Revolution in America* (1970).

2

Passive Resistance
1776–1865

I have seen enough of the miseries of war to wish it might never more have existence in the world, and that some other mode might be found out to settle the differences . . . of nations.

—Thomas Paine, 1791[1]

The achievements of the American Revolution, including its legacy to later generations, are important to any understanding of the American tradition of nonviolence. For many, perhaps most, of the democratic reforms in the colonies were the result of nonviolent direct action—boycotts, popular uprisings, civil disobedience, even the destruction of property (stamps and tea)—before a resort to arms. These achievements are important for at least two reasons: they help to define the distinctive nature of the Revolution and how it was accomplished; and they dramatize the relationship between philosophy and strategy, thought and action, as nonviolent means for social change came to occupy a significant place in the new nation's political discourse.

John Adams's remark, in a letter to Hezekiah Niles in 1818, suggests the importance of nonviolent direct action in the struggle for independence from Great Britain. "The real American Revolution . . . a radical change in principles, sentiments, and affections of the people," Adams said, was fought and won, not on the battlefield, but in the hearts and minds of the people.

As a lawyer who had defended British soldiers involved in the Boston Massacre, Adams spoke in this letter, perhaps, of his own "conversion" to the radical cause; but he reminds us, too, of what was accomplished through nonviolent means in the early stages of resistance—the pamphlet "wars" and popular uprisings throughout the colonies. Extralegal means of bringing about social change, though not encouraged, were accepted in certain circumstances and recognized as contributions to the public good. "The existence of such a tradition meant, more over, that the people, or, as their opponents said, the mob, entered the struggle with Britain as an established social force, not as an agency newly invented to serve the ends of radical leadership."[2]

As this tradition became less visible after the Revolution, the peace churches—Quakers, Mennonites, and Brethren—kept it alive, in their ongoing effort to bring about social change, including the end of slavery, without killing. Like the early Christians and some religious orders (Franciscans, for example, who took a pledge never to engage in war), members of the peace churches dedicated themselves to the counsel "Blessed are the peacemakers." Joined by other religious and some secular societies in a nonviolent quest, they "witnessed" their belief through various strategies: silent vigils, prayer meetings, and liturgies that focused on pacifist teachings. In this modest way, by refusing to take up arms for any cause or to pay taxes for them, they affirmed their commitment to the pacifist implications of Jesus' teachings within a political context. As advocates for peace, and eventually through the abolitionist movement, they recognized "the vision of love as an agent for fundamental social change," as Staughton Lynd later defined nonviolence.

Although initial efforts toward independence and some policies of the new nation reflected the influence of nonviolence, that influence declined soon afterward, particularly after the ratification of the Constitution in 1789 and through the period of the War of 1812. The change in attitude is reflected in the patriotic rhetoric of the period—a natural consequence of war. Nonviolence reemerged, in public discourse at least, only with the abolitionists after 1820.

Because of their experience with the British, the colonists, including delegates to the Constitutional Convention, had maintained a strong prejudice against standing armies. And in forming the new government, Benjamin Rush—author, earlier, of pamphlets on the cruelty of slavery—proposed a Peace Academy as one of the important national offices. It took two centuries, however, for the government to establish a special agency committed not to "making war" but to "making peace"; that event happened only during the waning years of the cold war, with the founding of the U.S. Institute of Peace.

In a related matter, James Madison proposed an amendment to the

Constitution (that is, the Bill of Rights) that would exclude anyone with religious scruples against war from having to bear arms or to perform military service. In the ensuing debate and eventual action by Congress, conscientious objection was included as a legislative *privilege* rather than a Constitutional *right;* any lawful alternative to military service, however, had to await the provision included in the conscription act of 1940.

Among the few pacifist writings provoked by the War of 1812, *The Lawfulness of War for Christians, Examined* (1814), by James Mott Sr., Quaker father-in-law of the great abolitionist and feminist Lucretia Mott, is the most notable. Acknowledging the writings of Erasmus, he dismissed justifications for taking up arms, on the basis of the Old Testament, as "but a fig-leaf covering."[3]

By 1815, however, peace societies existed in several states, the one in Massachusetts numbering one thousand members by 1822. Six years later, the state societies combined to form the American Peace Society. Three books indicate the general approach of such organizations and set the tone for a number of subsequent publications emphasizing its moral precepts: *The Mediator's Kingdom Not of This World: But Spiritual* (1809) and *War Inconsistent with the Religion of Christ* (1815), by David Low Dodge, a New York merchant; and *A Solemn Review of the Custom of War* (1814), by Noah Worcester, a Massachusetts Congregational minister. Dodge's books argued against war because it wastes human and natural resources and results in hatred and revenge, rather than peace and liberty. Worcester's book maintained that war never rights the wrong it addresses and kills the people least responsible for the policies that prompted the conflict. These moral treatises caught the attention of influential literary figures, including Ralph Waldo Emerson, who addressed the American Peace Society in 1838 on the topic of "War"; but they remain in the background, as the militant abolitionists assumed principal responsibility for social justice, emphasizing strategy as well as philosophy.

The period from 1830 to 1860, which spans the early lives, and the theoretical and practical essays of William Lloyd Garrison (1805–1879), Adin Ballou (1803–1890), and Elihu Burritt (1810–1879), is central to the American tradition of nonviolence in identifying major issues and concerns. Also during those decades, the major works by Hawthorne, Thoreau, and Whitman were published; although not advocates of nonviolence, in their writings, these writers reflected and contributed to the search for alternatives to violence during the formative years of American life and culture.

An extensive body of writings on nonviolence began with Garrison's straightforward response to a summons to serve in the state militia in 1829 (at roughly the same time as the emerging "renaissance" in American letters among transcendentalists and other Brahmins):

> I am not professedly a Quaker; but I heartily, entirely and practically embrace the doctrine of nonresistance, and am conscientiously opposed to all military exhibitions. I now solemnly declare that I will never obey any order to bear arms, but rather cheerfully suffer imprisonment and persecution.

Because the design of military training is to "make men *skillful murderers*," Garrison added, he could not "consent to become a pupil in this sanguinary school."[4]

Having formerly advocated colonization for black people, Garrison had by this time come under the influence of a mild-mannered Quaker, Benjamin Lundy. After coediting an important journal with him, Garrison parted ways with Lundy to pursue a more militant course as editor of *The Liberator* (1831–1865). Through the periodical, as well as through his speeches and personal witness, Garrison inspired and influenced many abolitionists and feminists, particularly Abigail Kelley Foster, editor of the *Anti-Slavery Bugle;* Angelina Grimke (younger sister of Sarah), whose "Appeal to the Christian Women of the South" first appeared in *The Liberator;* and Lucy Stone, editor of *Woman's Journal.* Other Garrisonians included Lydia Maria Child, poet and novelist; Frederick Douglass, former slave, editor of *North Star*—and with Sojourner Truth, the most influential African American abolitionist; and Ezra Heywood, a young radical, who later called *The Liberator* "the 'craziest' newspaper of that day."

Heywood wrote this testimony from jail, in 1892, after he and his wife, Angela Tilton, had turned to other reforms: the eight-hour day, free love, and a kind of free-speech movement in the manner of Berkeley students seventy years later. Yet it was *The Liberator* that had started Heywood "on the line of Anti-slavery, Woman's Rights and Peace."[5]

In a similar manner, several women abolitionists associated with Garrison became agitators for women's rights. In the case of the Grimke sisters and Lucretia Mott, their militant stand against slavery and discrimination provoked needed reforms within the Quaker community as well. Mott, among others, recognized the close association between the message (liberation) and the medium (nonresistance). "I am no advocate of passivity. Quakerism as I understand it does not mean quietism. The early

Friends were agitators, disturbers of the peace," she said, and she took it as a compliment when a friend called her "the most belligerent Non-Resistant he ever saw."[6] Lucy Stone, the first woman to speak from a pulpit in Massachusetts, came to the women's movement by way of abolitionism; as a student at Oberlin College, she had arranged for her friends Abigail Kelley Foster and Stephen Symonds Foster to speak—though Stone had to move the meeting to a nearby church when college authorities objected to "radicals" speaking on campus.

The central document of abolitionism and nonresistance was Garrison's "Declaration of Sentiments" (1838), adopted by the New England Non-Resistance Society after it broke away from the American Peace Society. In a letter to his wife, shortly after that event, Garrison accurately called it the most " 'fanatical' or 'disorganizing' instrument ever penned." Making no distinction among members of different rank or sex or national origin, the adopters of the Declaration reclaimed Paine's concept, "citizen of the world," and laid the groundwork for Tolstoy's Christian anarchism. In *The Kingdom of God is Within You* (1893), the great Russian novelist quoted Garrison extensively in his pamphlets on civil disobedience and nonviolence—as have later activists and philosophers of nonviolence:

> We register our testimony, not only against all war, whether offensive or defensive, but all preparations for war; . . . As every human government is upheld by physical strength, and its laws are enforced virtually at the point of the bayonet, we cannot hold any office which imposes upon its incumbent the obligation to do right, on pain of imprisonment or death.[7]

The document set a standard against which people advocating justice without resorting to violence might test themselves. Although Garrison based much of his argument on Christian teachings—"the old covenant" regarding "an eye for an eye, and a tooth for a tooth" had been abrogated by Jesus—Garrison and others have emphasized that their resistance to unjust laws is not based solely upon religious beliefs.

"Declaration of Sentiments" is also a great seedbed of ideas regarding the relationship between the individual and the state. In advocating the emancipation of slaves, an end to capital punishment, and abstention from conventional politics, it summarized the Christian anarchist position, which is more radical than that of most pacifists yet central to the tradition, from Tolstoy and the Dukhobors to Gandhi, Dorothy Day, and the Catholic Worker movement, as well as the Plowshares—Philip Berrigan and Elizabeth McAlister, Molly Rush, Carl Kabat, and Helen Woodson.

An impressive array of manifestos and essays of the nineteenth century shows a literary debt to "Declaration of Sentiments." Examples include Thoreau's "Civil Disobedience" (1848) and Ballou's *Practical Christian Socialism: A Conversational Exposition of the True System of Human Society* (1854) and *Christian Non-Resistance Defended Against Rev. Henry Ward Beecher* (1862). The literary reaction to it was also extensive, including the writings of Emerson, who remained sympathetic to "the dogma of no-government and non-resistance, and anticipated the objections and the fun," and of Hawthorne and Melville.[8]

Although both Garrison and Thoreau made substantial contributions to the nonviolent tradition through their writings, it should be added that neither was an absolute pacifist. Garrison gave nonresistance its shape and its drive, as Peter Brock has said, and narrowly escaped death at the hands of a mob in Boston in 1835. At that time, he insisted that he would "perish sooner than raise my hand against any man, even in self-defense," and wanted none of his friends to resort to violence to protect him.[9] Later, he compromised his antistatism and anarchism by throwing his support behind Lincoln's war and embracing the Union army's cause as a holy crusade. Thoreau, similarly, defended John Brown when the latter resorted to the use of arms in the antislavery struggle.

The Liberator nonetheless continued to print articles favoring nonviolence after the war began. Through it all, whatever his belief and change in attitude, Garrison lived according to the principles espoused in the first issue of *The Liberator:* "I am in earnest—I will not equivocate—I will not excuse—I will not retreat a single inch—*and I will be heard.*"

Such persistence characterized his agitation for women's rights, as well. In a famous incident in London, he sat in silent protest with women not allowed to speak in an international assembly. After battling so long to free the slaves, he argued, he would have nothing to do with a convention that ignored the rights of all women.

Although generally less well-known than Garrison, Adin Ballou, an advocate of abolitionism, women's rights, and nonresistance, is perhaps the most significant philosopher of nonviolence before Tolstoy—and a major figure, by the nature of his wisdom, modesty, and skills as a writer and communitarian, in American cultural history. Recognizing the controversial nature of his "unpopular doctrine," Ballou invariably spoke with confidence and openhandedness in exploring the full implications of nonresistance. Regarding it "as ancient as Christianity, and as true as the New Testament," he asks that "friends and opposers be candid, just and generous" of his exposition, approving or condemning it "solely on its own intrinsic merits and demerits."[10]

Born in 1803, two years before Garrison, in Cumberland, Rhode Island, Ballou traced his family to the early founders of that colony. His

writings in various periodicals were influential, first, among Unitarian/
Universalists—he had responded early to what he regarded as a supernatu-
ral call to its ministry. Saying he was "no antagonist to human government," Ballou nonetheless challenged the basic ideologies of the state,
capitalist or socialist, and pointed to injustices associated with "the whole
rotten system," as Dorothy Day would later call it:

> [It is] a system characterized by incessant rivalries and conflicting inter-
> ests, by artificial class distinctions and fierce antagonisms, by glaring
> extremes of wealth and poverty, of ease and slavish toil, of luxury and
> want, of happiness and misery, by manifold nurseries of iniquity, degra-
> dation, and shame, by gigantic military establishments, and vast engi-
> neering for slaughtering men and multiplying the sorrows of the world.

Speaking to a September 25, 1839, meeting of the Non-Resistance Society in Boston, Ballou addressed the question whether one must "disobey
parents, patriarchs, priests, kings, nobles, presidents, governors, generals,
legislatures, constitutions, armies, mobs, *all* rather than disobey God?"
His answer: "We *must;* and then patiently endure the penal consequences."

According to the constitution of the Hopedale community, which
Ballou cofounded in central Massachusetts in 1841, "no individual shall
suffer the evils of oppression, poverty, ignorance or vice through the
influence or neglect of others." And five years later in his famous book
entitled *Christian Non-Resistance,* Ballou listed the seven commandments
against war and capital punishment, much in the spirit of Garrison's Declaration, that conscientious followers of Jesus should obey.

In both his writing and his personality, Ballou's style resembled the
sweet reasonableness of Woolman more than the moralistic vigor of Garrison. Challenging the practicality of self-preservation, for example, he said
that if self-preservation is the best method of protecting and preserving
human life, why have "fourteen thousand millions of human beings been
slain by human means, in war and otherwise?" Might one not conclude
from such evidence that "self-preservation" is

> the off-spring of a purblind instinct—the cherished salvo of ignorance—
> the fatal charm of deluded credulity—the *supposed preserver,* but the *real
> destroyer* of the human family? . . . If the sword of self-defense had fright-
> ened the sword of aggression into its scabbard, there to consume in its
> rust; then might we admit that the common method of self-preservation
> was the true one.

On the other hand, if everyone since the conflict of Cain and Abel had responded to robbery, murder, and killing with nonresistance, Ballou asked, would as many lives have been sacrificed, or as much real misery have been experienced by the human race, "as has resulted from the usual method of responding to injury with injury?"[11] As with so many of Ballou's arguments and questions, such reflections seem as pertinent to any discussion of the just-war theory and nonviolence now as they were in his time. Perhaps that is because, as Peter Brock observed, Ballou, unlike many other philosophers of nonviolence, including Tolstoy, emphasized the relationship between theory and practice. And for all his utopianism, Ballou, like Burritt and others, "had at least one foot firmly grounded on the rocky New England soil."[12]

During his later life, Ballou watched as his friends and fellow nonresistants forgot or disavowed their earlier commitment to nonviolence. Elihu Burritt, on the other hand, Ballou's longtime associate and friend, continued to argue against violent means, even for a good cause, and explored strategies by which people might resist despotic rulers, while maintaining the battleword over their doorposts: *"No political change is worth a single crime, or a single drop of human blood."*[13] Of all those who devoted themselves to various causes of justice and peace in this period, in fact, none is more impressive than Burritt—worker, linguist, and pamphleteer. (Tradition, if not hard evidence, suggests that he was also the model for Henry Wadsworth Longfellow's popular poem, "The Village Blacksmith.")

Among Burritt's many contributions was an important essay, "Passive Resistance," in *Thoughts and Things at Home and Abroad* (1854), as well as his founding, with Ballou, of the world's first international peace society the same year, and his indefatigable pursuit, throughout North America and Western Europe in 1867, of a workers' agreement never to take up arms against their brothers and sisters again. Forty years before the founding of the Industrial Workers of the World (IWW), whose goals were similar, Burritt gathered tens of thousands of signatures on a petition encouraging workers to "make a universal and simultaneous *strike* against the whole war system." The effort represented an important direction and new strength among workers—an attempt at mass acts, rather than Thoreau's individual acts, on behalf of justice and peace.

Born in 1810, in New Britain, Connecticut, to a veteran of the Revolutionary War, Burritt shared a life of hardship with his parents and their large family. He apprenticed himself to a village blacksmith after the death of his father; and in the midst of his labors, he gained a love for poetry and soon delighted in the study of languages. By the time he was thirty, he had acquainted himself "with all the languages of Europe and several of Asia, including Hebrew, Syriac, Chaldaic, Samaritan, and Ethiopic."[14] Moving to Worcester, Massachusetts, he borrowed grammars and lexicons from the American Antiquarian Society there, continued his study, and eventually became known to Henry Wadsworth Longfellow, poet and professor of modern languages at Harvard University.

Offered opportunities for formal study and an appointment to Yale University, Burritt, as with Eugene Victor Debs later on, maintained that his vocation was "to stand in the ranks of the workingmen of New England, and beck-on them onward and upward . . . to the full stature of intellectual men." Along the way, Burritt published a periodical, *The Bond of Universal Brotherhood,* in the United States and in England, edited the journal of the American Peace Society, and was nominated for vice president on the working men's ticket. His many contributions to peace included popularizing the ideas of William Ladd (1778–1841), which later shaped the World Court and League of Nations, and helping to resolve a conflict over the Oregon Territory between the United States and Great Britain.

Stephen Symonds Foster, another faithful nonresistant, husband of the famous abolitionist Abigail Kelley Foster and author of the popular antislavery tracts *The Brotherhood of Thieves; or a True Picture of the American Church and Clergy* (1843), and *Revolution the Only Remedy for Slavery* (1855), took nonviolent direct action on several occasions. Jailed for owing twelve dollars and fourteen cents while a student at Dartmouth College, he caused such a furor about conditions in the prison that the town eventually cleaned it up; soon afterward, the New Hampshire legislature abolished imprisonment for debt. At Union Theological Seminary, he was offered a scholarship if he agreed to stop agitating for abolitionism. He left, in disgust, to become an itinerant preacher and controversialist.

During the famous Butman riot in 1854, in Worcester, Massachusetts, Foster placed himself between an angry mob and a federal marshall, who came to town to arrest a fugitive slave. A militant abolitionist, Foster was equally adamant against anyone's harming the marshall, who eventually left the city unharmed. In "Are Non-Resistants for Murder?" in response to John Brown's resorting to violence on the side of abolitionism, Foster sounds rather like Gandhi and Dorothy Day in condemning inaction in the face of injustice: "I claim to be a Non-Resistant, but not to be a fool," Foster said. "John Brown has shown himself a *man,* in comparison with the Non-Resistants."[15]

Stephen and Abby Foster also refused to pay taxes on their property as a protest against oppressive laws regarding women. They endeavored to understand how the concept of "passive resistance" informed every aspect of their lives, including their relationship as husband and wife. This was evident in their correspondence before their wedding—performed "on the run," during Abigail's speaking engagements in eastern Pennsylvania—and afterward, when Stephen cared for their daughter. On the road, Abigail scandalized her contemporaries by traveling with African American men and women.

In "Letter from Boston"—a series of portraits of his famous contemporaries, including Garrison, "his features very / Benign for an incendiary," and Wendell Phillips—James Russell Lowell compared Stephen Symonds Foster to "A kind of maddened John the Baptist / To whom the harshest word comes aptest," and Abigail Kelley Foster to

> A Judith, turned Quakeress
> . . . in her modest dress,
> Serving a table quietly
> As if that mild and downcast eye
> Flashed never, with its scorn intense,
> More than Medea's eloquence. . . .
> No nobler gift of heart and brain
> No life more white from spot or stain
> Was e'er on Freedom's alter laid
> Than hers—the simple Quaker maid.[16]

Editor of the *Anti-Slavery Bugle* and principal organizer of the second national women's convention, Abigail Kelley Foster lived her motto, "Go where you are least wanted, for there you are most needed," as a nonresistant, to the very end of a productive life. In a tribute to her at the time of her death, the great feminist Lucy Stone said that Abigail cleared a path over which many women walked to freedom. She had taken on her young shoulder "a double burden, for the slave's freedom, and for equal rights for women."[17]

Stone, who divided her week between abolitionism and feminism, working for the first on weekends and for the second Monday through Friday, also made many contributions to the nonviolent tradition, as did her husband, Henry Brown Blackwell. Even their wedding, in 1855, witnessed by Thomas Wentworth Higginson—militant abolitionist, clergyman, essayist, biographer, and editor—provided an occasion for protest. "While acknowledging our mutual affection by publicly assuming the relationship of husband and wife," Stone and Blackwell said in their marriage contract, "we deem it a duty to declare that this act on our part implies no sanction of, nor promise of voluntary obedience to such of the present laws of marriage, as refuse to recognize the wife as an independent, rational being." Thus did nonviolent resistance to oppression inform their lives, as it had the lives of Kelley and Foster; and after Stone and Blackwell died, their daughter, Alice Stone Blackwell (1857–1950), edited their influential *Woman's Journal* and remained an active feminist, as well as a member of the NAACP and the American Peace Society, well into the next century.

Other writers whose central themes are suggested by these titles from their collected works were C. K. Whipple, *Evils of the Revolutionary War* (1839) and *Non-Resistance Applied to the Internal Defense of a Community* (1860), and Henry C. Wright, *Defensive War Proved to Be a Denial of Christianity and the Government of God: With Illustrative Facts and Anecdotes* (1848). Anarchists who contributed to the nonviolent tradition included Josiah Warren, pamphleteer, editor of *The Peaceful Revolutionist* (1833), and critic of Robert Owen's New Harmony community; and Benjamin Tucker, whose "Relation of the State to the Individual" (1893) echoed Thoreau's "Civil Disobedience." Warren and Tucker were much concerned with issues regarding the conflict between the corporate state and individual conscience, as, of course, are many later activists and writers regarding war, conscription, and the international arms trade.

Just as the vitality of the abolitionist movement prepared the way for the great popular success of Harriet Beecher Stowe's *Uncle Tom's Cabin; or, Life Among the Lowly* (1852) and shortly afterward *Dred; A Tale of the Great Dismal Swamp* (1856/66), the strength of the nonresistant movement helps to account for Nathaniel Hawthorne's and, to a lesser degree, Herman Melville's preoccupation with—if not their skepticism toward—reformers in this period. Of the latter two major figures, Hawthorne was more sophisticated and skilled politically, which is one reason that his books remain among the most insightful critiques and "properties" of nonviolence. As an interpreter and critic of the American experience that had shaped him, he had a profound understanding of the peculiarities of the society, its traditions, and its political weaknesses and strengths. Several of Hawthorne's stories and novels might carry the title of Thoreau's Concord lecture, "On the Relation Between the Individual and the State," which the world knows as "Civil Disobedience," because Hawthorne's stories indicate as much sensitivity to the implications of social reform as do Thoreau's more obviously "political" essays.

Melville, on the other hand, appears to have understood the concept of nonviolence—or attitudes associated with it—hardly at all. His treatment of nonviolence, as embodied in the passive behavior of Bartleby in *Bartleby the Scrivener* (1853), is a caricature, rather than a convincing portrait of a true nonresistant. Bartleby's oft-repeated phrase, "I prefer not to"—without elaboration, reasons, or background information—may be regarded as merely peculiar. His behavior is the antithesis of the nonviolent activist's patient, labored effort to define terms and to outline varying perspectives—in helping others to identify, whenever possible, with his or her cause.

As an artist, Melville appeared to distance himself from many of the questions associated with social reform, including nonviolent direct action. Or so a later story, *Billy Budd,* suggests. Innocent, almost an angel, Billy Budd remains passive in the face of injustice, and his last cry, "God bless Captain Veer," belongs more to melodrama than to the complex requirements of action aimed at eventual reconciliation. Nor are Melville's stories likely to concern themselves with the difference between those committed to violent, and those committed to nonviolent, means.

Hawthorne's stories, by contrast, elucidate and play about several important themes and central concerns of nonviolence. Judging from his stories and novels, a reader might rightly look to Hawthorne as someone with deep understanding of and sensitivity to essential issues associated with building and sustaining a civil society. For in spite of Hawthorne's innate conservatism, in *The House of the Seven Gables* (1851) and in *The Blithedale Romance* (1852), he creates some of the most fully rendered nonresistants available in fiction. They are lifelike and recognizable in ways that characters affected by similar political or social forces, in the fiction of more committed reformers, are not.

Although somewhat naïve, Hawthorne's characters maintain a capacity for reconciliation—not just for obstinate defiance or a dramatic, romantic gesture—that reminds one of activists from the seventeenth century to the present, from John Woolman and Adin Ballou to Dorothy Day and Martin Luther King. Hawthorne's reformers are not just obstinate and defiant, in other words, or given only to dramatic, romantic gestures; they sense their place in the larger culture and sometimes achieve a kind of reconciliation with it. Although they never quite "alter" the world, it does respond to their presence in the ultimate assimilation of their character into the wider realm.

Before turning to specific examples, it may be appropriate here to say something about the way Hawthorne's "politics" has been stripped of all meaning by earlier critical preoccupation with everything but his social themes and images. Few American writers, in fact, have been so consciously political in their fiction, and anyone attempting to understand the resistance to political change in the United States is wise to attend to the powerful conservative rhetoric of this great writer.

In story after story, Hawthorne is much more concerned with the social implications of his characters' rebelling—Hester Prynne's in *The Scarlet Letter* (1850), for example—than he is with the moral or religious implications of sin. Sacvan Bercovitch rightly calls that novel "thick propaganda," in its advocacy of "a world view," a "metaphysics of choosing," within which a particular course of action "makes sense and takes effect." [18] One might regard *The House of the Seven Gables,* similarly, as a metaphysics of "conflict resolution," American style. Although his angle of vision on social struggle or revolution differs from that of the nonresistants—and of Emerson, Thoreau, and Margaret Fuller—Hawthorne was every bit as preoccupied with issues related to theirs.

Like earlier American writers Washington Irving and James Fenimore Cooper, Hawthorne was suspicious of the "revolutionary" aspirations of his contemporaries. In his friendships as well as in his fiction, Hawthorne indicated a distinct unease with reformers—feminists, abolitionists, even transcendentalists—of his day, a characteristic that complicated his relationships with Thoreau and Emerson; the latter wrote in his journal, for example, of Hawthorne's "perverse politics and unfortunate friendship with that paltry Franklin Pierce." Miles Coverdale, in *The Blithedale Romance,* may speak for one side of the author's character when he says, "I seriously wished . . . that the reformation of society had been postponed about half a century, or at all events, to such a date as should have put my intermeddling with it entirely out of the question."

In overemphasizing Hawthorne's long seclusion as an apprentice writer and his personal reticence among the more talkative Concord literati, readers and critics sometimes forget the significance of Hawthorne's public life. Read beside his notebooks, his stories and novels reveal the close relationship between his dominant aesthetic and the highly political nature of his moral tales. By 1845, as his biographer, James R. Mellow, has said, Hawthorne "had acquired the talent for rationalization by which political careers were sustained," and had cast his lot with the conservative wing of the Democratic Party;[19] shortly afterward, Hawthorne wrote a campaign biography for his old friend Franklin Pierce, with its strong criticism of the abolitionist movement. As the English critic Edward Dicey said, "The whole nature of Hawthorne shrank from the rough wear and tear inseparable from great popular movements of any kind," and "the details of a popular agitation were strangely offensive to him."

Hawthorne's daughter Rose, later a Dominican nun and founder of hospitals for the terminally ill, spoke about her father's hatred of "disorder,

broken rules, and weariness of discipline." Is it any wonder that the casu-
alness of Brook Farm, which resulted in his loss of considerable savings,
upset Hawthorne and that the "right" way to live, in his fiction, is often
with the status quo, rather than in those utopian ventures so dear to many
nineteenth-century reformers? Anyone challenging the accepted order of
things was likely to find himself or herself roundly criticized, even satirized, in a Hawthorne story.

Holgrave, for example, the young anarchist in *The House of the Seven
Gables,* is Hawthorne's characteristic nonresistant. Handsome, intelligent,
good natured, Holgrave nonetheless betrays a certain lack of decorum by
wearing blousy shirts and consorting with political radicals—"anarchists"
—before his meeting Phoebe. As his "education" proceeds in the novel,
he gradually learns more sensible behavior and ultimately understands his
place in society—in relation to older people, the surrounding community,
and the woman he loves. In a famous scene, when Holgrave renounces his
hypnotic power over Phoebe, the reader gets some sense of Hawthorne's
solution to social unrest. In order for society to heal itself, he implies, a
personal renunciation of violence must precede any social movement for
change. Only after Holgrave's abdication of his power over Phoebe are
the two warring families united; only then are the two young people able
to make a new beginning, unburdened by the weight of old curses, old
conflicts, old fears.

Hawthorne, disillusioned by the Brook Farm experiment and allied
politically with moderate democrats, including Pierce and others less militant on the slavery issue, remained skeptical of all reformers throughout
his life. He was fascinated, nonetheless, by rebels—Anne Hutchinson, the
early Quakers, as well as Hester Prynne, Hollingsworth, Zenobia—and as
preoccupied with the threat of violence in American culture as Garrison
and Thoreau were.

As with the nonresistants, Hawthorne possessed a remarkable awareness of the many forces affecting the social order and the difficulty of
balancing them in the interest of a truly civil society. Time and again, he
worried over the consequences of disruption and the dangers it posed to
the "new" America. Remembering that he was born only thirty years after
the founding of the new nation and lived through incidents that threatened its survival, one may sympathize, in part, with his general conservative outlook. More than the nonresistants, one might say, Hawthorne was
aware of the threats to peace posed by the mercantile class, including
professionals like the Pyncheons, who stole and wheedled their way to
wealth and power. They, as with the dreamers, abstract thinkers, and
reformers, among whom is the handsome and generous Holgrave, need

the calming, refined influence of a sensible Phoebe in order to become better citizens.

The House of the Seven Gables may be regarded as a classic text in the nonviolent tradition because it treats, argues, and anticipates whole areas of concern important to nonviolent strategists and philosophers: how to resist humiliation, how to resolve conflict, how to accommodate people of radically different ideologies in the same society, how the criminal justice system itself perpetuates injustice, and more.

Very different from Hawthorne's attitude, yet equally central to the tradition of nonviolence, are the personal and public ruminations of Thoreau. Although he regarded himself as a mystic and natural philosopher, he has probably pushed more people into action than have most so-called revolutionaries, violent or nonviolent. In his forty-five years, he ventured from his native town, Concord, Massachusetts, only occasionally; but like his contemporary Emily Dickinson of Amherst, he learned more from his relatively circumscribed life than most people learn by traveling the world.

Younger than most of the central figures of this period, Thoreau mined the secrets of nonviolence, it appears, somewhat as he mined the secrets of nature, in the laboratory nearby: among his transcendentalist friends and neighbors, as well as at Walden Pond. And his writings have long provided a vigorous, authoritative, and inspiring rationale for resisting the warmaking state.

Over the past hundred years, Thoreau's writings have also brought thousands of people very different from him to nonviolence: Tolstoy, Gandhi, Ammon Hennacy, Martin Luther King, as well as Danes resisting Nazis during the Second World War and Chinese students waging the 1989 uprising. Of course, the added irony is that even Thoreau justified killing in the struggle for justice.

In a strategic sense, Thoreau's central insight may be that those responsible for evil—in his time, for slavery—succeed not because of their commitment, but because others who recognize the evil do nothing to resist it. "Practically speaking, the opponents of a reform in Massachusetts are not a hundred thousand politicians in the South, but a hundred thousand merchants and farmers here, who are more interested in commerce and agriculture than they are in humanity." Reading the essay "Civil Disobedience," one recognizes his argument as still one of the best for confronting the politics of greed or the violence of the status quo that precedes the collapse of the social order.

A related and central point of "Civil Disobedience," and Thoreau's later defense of John Brown, is that citizens will not have a better society merely by wishing for it. "Even voting for the right is doing nothing for it. It is only expressing to men feebly your desire that it should prevail." Writing in his journal about the same time, Thoreau said of tepid citizens, "Better are the physically dead for they more lively rot." George Orwell's insistence, in "Politics and the English Language," that having no opinion about public issues is itself a political decision echoes Thoreau's emphasis upon "doing something."

Although not the first effort advocating resistance to a system that upheld slavery and other policies associated with imperialism, "Civil Disobedience" brought those arguments together in a particularly eloquent, economical manner. Profiting from and building upon similar statements by Garrison, Ballou, and Bronson Alcott—who went to jail before Thoreau—he directed his challenge at friends and neighbors, including Emerson, for their failure to take a more militant stand against injustice. Although Thoreau was not a pacifist, his essay remains, along with the Declaration of Independence and Martin Luther King's "Letter from Birmingham Jail," the most influential document in the American tradition of nonviolence.

A recent publication associated with the growing movement for conscientious objection to war tax, including pending legislation in Congress, for example, focuses on "Civil Disobedience." Prominent in the War Resister's League tax resistance publications, and echoed in Allen Ginsberg's statement supporting tax refusal during the Vietnam War, is this quotation:

> If a thousand men were not to pay their tax-bills this year, that would not be a violent and bloody measure, as it would be to pay them, and enable the State to commit violence and shed innocent blood. This is, in fact the definition of a peaceable revolution if any such is possible.

Reading "Civil Disobedience," one cannot help thinking that no contemporary writer of Thoreau's stature, religious, philosophical, or literary, speaks with his moral clarity and vigor on principled resistance to injustice.

In a general way, the writings and the person of Walt Whitman, as indicated in the Preface, belong to this history as well. Fired from his job as editor of the Brooklyn *Eagle* for his strong editorials against slavery, Whitman was the natural ally of anyone confronting injustice and suffering in a nonviolent way. Conflicted, contradictory, self-dramatizing, he contributed to the struggle for justice in the best way he knew how, that is, through his poems. He built on the Quaker legacy that he inherited from his parents and that he referred to often in his early life. He treasured a meeting with Thomas Paine, that "citizen of the world" whom his father had known, and as an old man and a public figure, spoke on anniversaries associated with Paine.

Although some Civil War poems in *Leaves of Grass* and his memorable tributes to Lincoln, particularly "When Lilacs Last in the Dooryard Bloom'd," sound conventionally patriotic, even nationalistic, Whitman argued strongly, in many poems and statements about his work, for reconciliation among enemies and antagonists. In several poems—and certainly in his actions—he provides a powerful example of the nonviolent ethic, sacrificing his health and taking risks himself for the ideas he believed in. Drawn to the Civil War battlefield when his brother was wounded, Whitman remained there as a nurse for four years, endangering his own health and providing essential care for soldiers from the South as well as from the North.

Quotations that have become part of the literature of nonviolence include the brief poem "To These States," among "Inscriptions," at the beginning of *Leaves of Grass:*

> *Resist much, obey little,*
> Once unquestioning obedience, once fully enslaved.

He defined the proper attitude of great poets, "to cheer up slaves and horrify despots," in the 1855 Preface, just before offering this straightforward and practical advice regarding "what you shall do":

> Love the earth and sun and the animals, despise riches, give alms to every one that asks, stand up for the stupid and crazy, devote your income and labor to others, hate tyrants, argue not concerning God, have patience and indulgence toward the people, take off your hat to nothing known or unknown or to any man or number of men, go freely with powerful uneducated persons and with the young and with the mothers of families, read these leaves in the open air every year of your life, re-examine all you have been told at school or church or in any book, dismiss whatever insults your own soul, and your very flesh shall be a great poem and have the richest fluency not only in its words but in the silent lines of its lips and face and between the lashes of your eyes and in every motion and joint of your body.

That sound and sense, that simplicity and directness, not to mention the statement's radical implications, set the tone for numerous similar encomiums in American writing, most notably anarchist sentiments, as in Peter Maurin's "Easy Essays" and Paul Goodman's *Drawing the Line*

(1965), as well as in similar tracts by radicals and environmentalists such as Scott and Helen Nearing.

One of Whitman's hopes for the "voice" in *Leaves of Grass,* noted earlier, was that "before me all the armies and soldiers of the earth shall yet bow—and all the weapons of war become impotent." Although he later deleted these lines, they reflect Whitman's feelings about a tension between his overall purpose in writing his book and that of earlier epic poets.

Appropriately, given his Quaker heritage, Whitman regarded the subject of war in poetry as problematic; and he addressed this thematic concern—as he addressed stylistic concerns about rhyme and meter—in a new and direct way. "As I Pondered," for example, the second "inscription" in *Leaves of Grass,* records a conversation between the author and "A Phantom . . . , / Terrible in beauty, age, and power," who confronts him about his choice of subject:

> *Know'st thou not there is but one theme for ever-enduring bards?*
> *And that is the theme of War. . . .*

"Be it so," the narrator answers, then explains his angle of vision on the matter. As with Homer in the *Iliad,* Virgil in the *Aeneid,* and Milton in *Paradise Lost,* Whitman will indeed "sing war," he says, but not the "war" celebrated by his predecessors. He chronicles, instead, that battle "longer and greater," the battle waged on "the field of the world," rather than on a national battlefield. He will promote "brave soldiers" of a different kind, chanting, instead,

> Of Life immense in passion, pulse, and power, . . .
> *For Life and death, for the Body and for the eternal Soul.*

This interior struggle, with profound religious overtones, involves "the Female equally with the Male."

With the example of George Fox and John Woolman in the background, Whitman's autobiographical musings anticipated those of later writers and activists, from Gandhi to Barbara Deming, Muriel Rukeyser, and Allen Ginsberg. As *Leaves of Grass* grew and changed from 1855, through the Civil War editions, to the ninth or deathbed edition of 1892, Whitman spoke increasingly not of triumph and defeat or of winners and losers, but of reconciliation—"word above all . . . beautiful as the sky," as he says in a poem from one of the later editions.

In the gradual unfolding of *Leaves of Grass,* it was as if Whitman, as with other activists and writers in the tradition who shared the Civil War years, understood the difficulties that advocates of nonviolence inevitably face in offering alternatives to war. Among them were the need for pacifists to decide "what must be done" regarding a military draft when, in 1863, the United States initiated national conscription. And what of the massive slaughter that followed, in spite of the vitality and imagination so many had shown in taking a moral stand against war and in devising various ways of resisting the state?

Perhaps because of these contradictions, there is still much to be learned about nonviolence from literary artifacts of this period and from writers who advocated and participated in movements for social change and those who resisted it, for various reasons. Is it mere coincidence that one of the most vital periods in our literary history—1840 to 1860— coincided with a time of major breakthroughs in nonviolent theory and strategy? That question is worth keeping in mind, also, as we turn to the years associated with the birth of modernism and the beginning of the First World War.

3

Labor Agitation and Religious Dissent
1865–1914

Would you have wings up in heaven to fly,
And starve here with rags on your back?

—Joe Hill[1]

The Civil War undermined—one might even say decimated—the nonviolent movement in the United States, so that it was some years before nonresistance, as it was then called, reclaimed a significant place in American history and literature. Although philosophers and strategists, particularly Garrison and Ballou, had deepened and extended the theoretical base of nonviolence, for the next half-century, Americans provided only limited leadership in the movement. A more conventional explanation, by an academic historian, describes the period in this way: "From the end of the Civil War to the close of the nineteenth century, the physical energies of the American people had been mobilized for a remarkable burst of material development, but their moral energies had lain relatively dormant."[2]

Faithful to their earlier teachings and preachings, even as the Civil War ended, Ballou, Burritt, and Ezra Heywood cofounded the Universal Peace Society in Boston, on December 12, 1865. Though pale in comparison with the Garrisonian leadership of previous years, it remained an important expression of pacifism over the next fifty years.

Among the three activists, Ezra Heywood (1829–1893) and his preoccupations suggest the new directions taken by nonviolent activists in the post-Civil War period. A generation younger than Ballou and Burritt, Heywood (née Hoare) was descended from a well-known New England family. Although he accused the established church of "hourly crucifying the Son of God afresh," his thinking reflected the early influence of evangelical Protestantism—as well as his father's sound advice: "Whenever you speak, say what you think regardless of other's opinions, commands or action; the fear of a man bringeth a snare."[3]

Two feminist abolitionists—whom he met while attending Brown University—drew Heywood into the abolitionist cause, as well as to the women's movement. Although he regarded the Civil War as "just," initially, he later compared waging war to put down slavery to "lying to put down falsehood" or "stealing to put down theft," and denounced the military draft as "essentially wicked and despotic, to be disobeyed and trod under foot."

In 1865, Heywood married Angela Tilton, who shared his commitment to feminism, free love, labor reform, and nonviolence. His many publications, in addition to translations of the Russian anarchist Michael Bakunin, included *Uncivil Liberty* (1870), arguing for woman's suffrage, and *Cupid's Yokes* (1876), promoting "sexual health and purity." The latter book, along with his periodical *The Word*, provoked the ire of Anthony Comstock and led to Heywood's two lengthy prison terms because of his frank discussions of sexuality and birth control. Although he refused to condemn workers who resisted injustice with violence, Heywood remained faithful to nonresistance, saying in *The Great Strike* (1877), for example, "I would not take another's life to save my own." He, like Ballou, concerned himself with the strategy as well as the philosophy of nonviolence; and he had plans to lecture on "Nonresistant Soldiers; or, The New Order, Which Refusing to Fire on the Strikers, Heralds," before going to jail.[4]

While a few people continued to uphold "forgotten visions, lost utopias, unfulfilled dreams," as Howard Zinn calls them, American writers were generally less interested in nonviolent social change after the Civil War than they were in the previous period. Activists and authors in other countries instead dominated discussions about the philosophy and strategy of resisting injustice and resolving conflict while refusing to kill.

Beginning in the 1880s, the Russian novelist Leo Tolstoy (1828–1910) furthered the cause of Christian anarchism and nonviolence, building upon what he had learned from the writings of Ballou, Garrison, Burritt, and Thoreau. In the 1890s, in South Africa, Mohandas Gandhi, after reading Tolstoy, initiated major campaigns against laws that humiliated Indians and other minorities; there, Gandhi founded Tolstoy Farm and in 1915 returned to India, where he took up the campaign against British rule. Before and after the turn of the century, Tolstoy's writings influenced several well-known Americans, as they began to address the plight of immigrants and workers in this country, and the implications of American imperialism in the Caribbean and the Pacific Rim.

Leo Tolstoy, following his conversion to radical Christianity about 1880, gave the tradition of nonviolence, including civil disobedience, a rich body of literature: first, with *The Kingdom of God Is Within You* (1893–94) and then, with pamphlets and public letters up to the time of his death in 1910. Tolstoy risked jail himself in supporting draft resisters and pacifists, such as the Dukhobors, whose exile to Canada was financed in part by royalties from his writings, particularly *Resurrection* (1910). The same vigor and intelligence that had made Tolstoy, through his novels and stories, the most famous writer in the world, gave weight and resonance to his pamphlets against "war" in every form.

In "The Inevitable Revolution," posthumously published, he repeated a central argument of his writings on nonviolence, that "the thief who steals and the richman, amassing and maintaining wealth, and the ruler, signing the death sentence, and the executioner carrying it out, and the revolutionary throwing a bomb, . . . and the soldier shooting at whomever he is ordered to, . . . do what they do only because they live according to a false belief in the [inevitability] of violence, . . . which can be destroyed only by each man freeing himself from this baneful superstition."[5] By his example, giving up his aristocratic advantages and counseling draft resistance and noncooperation with imperial governments in his writings, he continues to exert a profound influence on anyone committed to nonviolence.

As a radical Christian who was eventually excommunicated by the Russian Orthodox Church, Tolstoy blamed the decline of Christianity after Constantine on the church's failure to remain faithful to the pacifist teachings of Jesus and to dissociate itself from political power. In his most important pamphlets, Tolstoy quoted long passages from William Lloyd Garrison's early writings on civil disobedience and nonviolence. In "A Message to the American People" (1901), Tolstoy thanked the American people for their apostles of nonviolence, particularly the Quakers and those abolitionists who flourished in the 1850s, then chided Americans for paying too little attention to them and urged others to continue the good work in which abolitionists and antistatists "had made such hopeful progress."

Tolstoy strengthened the tradition, in other words, directly through several American writers and indirectly through Mohandas Gandhi—who read English translations of Tolstoy's *Kingdom of God Is Within You* and other pamphlets on nonviolence as early as 1894. About the same time,

William Jennings Bryan, Jane Addams, Clarence Darrow, and Ernest Howard Crosby made the pilgrimage to Tolstoy's home, Yasnaya Polyana. And it was common among reformers, according to Hamlin Garland, the popular American short story writer and essayist, to look to "Ibsen to reform the drama and Tolstoy to reform society."

The real impact of Tolstoy's teachings on nonviolence and Christian anarchism, however, became evident as the United States moved closer and closer to engagement in the First World War. As Britain lured the United States into active participation, socialists and pacifists cited Tolstoy's warnings about the state. And eventually, the British poet Wilfred Owen (1893–1918) had a cultural impact like no other writer, American or otherwise. He learned about Tolstoy while living in the household of his French translator, near Bordeaux, and made drawings of wounded soldiers returning from the western front as the war began. Upon entering the war as a soldier himself, Owen wrote poems that ridiculed the rhetoric of war; and his greatest poems, including "Dulce et Decorum Est" and "Le Christianisme," echoed, in language and rhetoric, Tolstoy's writings on nonviolence.

In the United States, during the last decade of the nineteenth century, William Jennings Bryan (1860–1925), influential orator, three-time nominee for president, and later secretary of state, regarded himself as a Tolstoyan, and with several major American writers—Mark Twain, William Dean Howells, and William James—supported the Anti-Imperialist League during the Spanish-American War. Twenty years later, as Woodrow Wilson became increasingly partisan toward one side in the European war, Bryan resigned as secretary of state because he disagreed with the administration's policy.

Clarence Darrow (1857–1938), criminal lawyer and civil libertarian, wrote *Resist Not Evil* (1903), based upon Tolstoy's teachings, and skillfully defended labor agitators and others in upholding basic human rights and democratic principles. In his pamphlet, "Marx vs. Tolstoi," published by Eugene Victor Debs's Appeal to Reason Press, Darrow argued that nonviolence—through determination, nonresistance, and peaceful force—promised the only kind of victory worth having. Although the First World War led to Darrow's abandoning pacifism, his reflections on nonviolence provide some insight regarding theories and strategies about power that have been more thoroughly studied by others.

Jane Addams (1860–1935), founder of Hull House and the Women's International League for Peace and Freedom, was deeply impressed by Tolstoy during her visit to Russia in 1896, although his eating peasant porridge and black bread—while his guests dined in style—made her uncomfortable. Addams, after searching for a vocation, had moved into the Italian ghetto of Chicago several years before her visit to Russia. There, with a group of educated women, she provided refuge for battered women and abandoned children and initiated an impressive program of education and the arts for the surrounding community, three-fourths of whom were foreign born.

Gradually, Addams came to recognize the relationship between injustice and violence, and the influence of Hull House extended to movements for child labor laws and better working conditions. She joined the Anti-Imperialist League during the Spanish-American War, and she supported various nongovernmental organizations committed to world peace.

When war broke out in Europe in August 1914, Addams argued that the United States should remain neutral. Like Bertrand Russell in England, Clarence Darrow, and Randolph Bourne, she thought the United States could best use its influence for arbitration between the Great Powers—Germany and Austria-Hungary—and the Allies—England, France, and Russia. In an early attempt to intervene directly on behalf of peace, she traveled at considerable personal risk to the western front, hoping to force political leaders to the bargaining table and thus end the war.

When the United States entered the war in 1917, Addams joined Debs, Bourne, and others emphasizing the disastrous effects of Wilson's policy, including the dangers of endorsing it uncritically. Looking back on this period, Addams in 1922 gave another reason for remaining faithful to the pacifist ethic in the midst of war. She thought that even a small number maintaining an unequivocal position served the cause of peace, however lonely and misunderstood they might be.

In her life and writings, Addams took Tolstoy's nonviolence ethic to heart and embodied it more fully herself than any other American. Combining a commitment to the poor and to nonviolence, that is, to justice and to peace, she held on to basic principles that few understood at a time of "total" war. By announcing herself a pacifist in 1915, she provoked criticisms from some of her principal admirers, including former President Theodore Roosevelt. Although he had been happy to have her second his nomination for president in 1912, as a third party candidate, he came to regard her just three years later as "the most dangerous woman in America." In some ways he was right, for her effectiveness in building alternative "peace" communities, while protesting U.S. intervention in Europe, amounted to a powerful legacy that future imperialists tried, but failed, to "read out of history."

Addams's education as a nonviolent activist had begun during her involvement with the more conservative, conventional testimony of the

American Peace Society, dating from the early nineteenth century. Its program for ending war leaned toward visionary proposals—broad and undefined—rather than practical proposals. Important to, but hardly elemental in shaping, the nonviolent tradition, "peace reform" centered on international relations, particularly arbitration, international law, and organization. Its constituency was decidedly upper-middle-class, building on Anglo-American relations and seldom challenging the political leadership or the imperial ambitions of either country. Instead, the American Peace Society tended to trust traditional diplomacy, and focused on initiatives such as the Hague Conferences, founded by Czar Nicholas II in 1899, and "the rules" of war.

Related organizations, sometimes well funded by robber barons of the period, included the World Peace Foundation and the Carnegie Endowment for International Peace, both founded in 1910, and the Church Peace Union (1914). These developments took place amid a mounting arms race, the expansion of colonial empires, and growing injustices against workers in a pattern that characterized "globalization from above" in the new century. Efforts at peace reform often collapsed when tested against traditional diplomacy, as a few rich and powerful men—their corporations protected by Supreme Court rulings—built, at the expense of the many, vast empires of wealth at home and abroad.

Until the First World War, peace societies seldom discussed the relationship between international initiatives (e.g., the World Court) and national campaigns against imperialism (e.g., the Anti-Imperialist League). Even as the U.S. government intervened or crushed movements for independence in Latin America and Asia, the American Peace Society, for example, continued to believe that global harmony could best be achieved through "elite education of the masses at home and the Christian disciplining of backward peoples abroad," as Charles DeBenedetti has said.[6] Such abstract, not to say misguided, approaches to "peace reform" provoked disillusionment among people facing a century of total war.

Despite popular indifference to social reform during post-Civil War industrialization, workers made important contributions to nonviolence, especially after 1885. Finding that they had little bargaining power individually, they formed broader associations, experimented with strategies for winning better wages and working conditions, and dramatized, for many people, the practicality and wisdom of nonviolent direct action. Writers sympathized with their plight and described it, but with only a limited sense of the issues involved or of alternatives for social change.

Various individuals and groups took bold initiatives, however, following the "great" Chicago strike of 1877 that Ezra Heywood wrote about, and especially after the founding of the American Federation of Labor and the 1886 Haymarket incident in Chicago. Workers—including Albert Parsons, who was an abolitionist before becoming a labor agitator and one of the "Haymarket martyrs"—had begun to emphasize the relationship between Negro slavery before the Civil War and the postwar wage slavery that replaced it. Active in labor organizing, Parsons was among the anarchists arrested in May of 1886, after a bomb exploded at Haymarket Square during a mass protest of workers. Although charges against them were never proved, four men were executed; later, Governor John Peter Altgeld pardoned the others. This incident radicalized the existing leadership, as well as those who followed, and evoked a library of poems, novels, memoirs, and songs sympathetic to social change, by Hamlin Garland, William Dean Howells, Robert Herrick, Frank Norris, Rebecca Harding Davis, and Upton Sinclair.

During the 1890s and into the first decade of the new century, novelists and muckraking journalists described the plight of workers graphically and sympathetically, particularly those among the rapidly increasing immigrant population. Howells's *Hazard of New Fortunes* (1890) and *A Traveler from Altruria* (1894), for example, dramatized the growing conflict between those who owned and ruled and those who worked and endured. And a sequel to the latter book, *Through the Eye of the Needle* (1907), provided a vision of a more just and equitable society, including some insight into the consequences of squandering the country's resources on a military budget. Although Howells remained an outspoken critic of American foreign policy, his insights into the psychological implications of the labor struggle and the sociological means of waging it were limited. His understanding of conflict centered primarily on questions of money, rather than of political power. Thus, his politics resembled other one-dimensional proposals for social change—such as Henry George's single tax plan—and for "what must be done."

From the Civil War to the First World War, then, problem solving and power struggles generally rewarded the rich and the privileged, at the expense of poorly paid workers, as immigrants poured into the United States from around the globe. American novelists and poets, with notable exceptions, offered little insight into the dynamics of social change in the way that Hawthorne did during the abolitionist period or that John Dos Passos, F. Scott Fitzgerald, and William Faulkner would do for the post-World War generation. One must turn, as I have already suggested, to other forms of written discourse—memoirs, songs, and pamphlets—to understand developments in the history of nonviolence during this period.

Gradually, however, major literary figures joined the small chorus of those alerted to the dangers of "imperial America." Howells, Mark Twain, and William James, among others, had been outraged by propaganda justifying murderous policies, as the United States gained control over or seized territories throughout the Pacific. Purchasing the Philippines from Spain at the end of the Spanish-American War gave the United States control only over Manila and its suburbs, though native forces had already liberated much of the rest of the country from Spain.

Over the next three years, 1899 to 1902, the United States managed to crush the popular, but poorly armed, Filipino forces and to abolish their republic. The estimated dead numbered one hundred thousand Filipinos, in a war that "lasted longer, involved more U.S. troops, cost more lives and had a more significant impact on the United States than the three-month Spanish-American War that preceded it."[7] This pattern played itself out as the United States annexed Hawaii, Puerto Rico, Guam, and the Panama Canal shortly afterward and eventually gained control over the Pacific, for reasons baldly stated by a U.S. senator at the time: "And just beyond the Philippines are China's illimitable markets. We will not retreat from either. . . . We will not abandon our opportunity in the Orient. We will not renounce our part in the mission of our race, trustee under God, of the civilization of the world."[8]

In its irregular and periodic battles against people of color in the Pacific and in Central America, the United States employed tactics long associated with imperial expansion. An inquiry by Secretary of War Elihu Root substantiated charges of American atrocities in the Philippines, where "U.S. armed forces had habitually tortured rebel suspects, shot prisoners or unlucky civilians, and burned and looted conquered areas."[9]

Mark Twain's parody of the "Battle Hymn of the Republic," written (though never published) in 1901, is representative of the literary response to such policies. As with several of his later short stories, the verse satirized the American hubris that motivated such policies, including the government's protection of prostitution in Manila:

> Mine eyes have seen the orgy of the launching of the Sword;
> He is searching out the hoardings where the stranger's
>   wealth is stored;
> He hath loosed his fateful lightnings,
>   and with woe and death has scored;
> His lust is marching on. . . .
> In a sordid slime harmonious,
>   Greed was born in yonder ditch,
> With a longing in his bosom—and for other's good an itch—
> As Christ died to make men holy,
>   let men die to make us rich—
> Our god is marching on.[10]

Six years before, when an editor at *Harper's Bazaar* rejected his famous "War Prayer," prompted by his concerns about American intervention in the Philippines and King Leopold's in the Belgian Congo, Twain wrote in his notebook, "In America—as elsewhere—free speech is confined to the dead."

At the time of his death in 1910, the Anti-Imperialist League, which Twain served as vice president for many years, praised him as not only "a brilliant humorist" but also "a passionate and zealous reformer." Although not a pacifist, Twain contributed to the increasing skepticism of writers and intellectuals regarding American imperialism. His influence is evident in the writings of two young socialists—Van Wyck Brooks and Randolph Bourne—who emphasized the importance of Twain's later writings in their literary criticism during the next decade.

If parts of Twain's "Mysterious Stranger" "aren't as blinding satire on the human comedy as anything Swift ever wrote," Bourne wrote in 1918, "then I am a fanatical pacifist, completely obsessed by the imbecility of wars and ready to judge any book great which ridicules human conflict."[11] In his influential, posthumously published essay "History of a Literary Radical," Bourne looked to Twain as the inspiration for a "new classicism" of "abounding vitality and moral freedom" that would combine "power with restraint, vitality with harmony, a fusion of intellect and feeling, and a keen sense of the artistic conscience."[12]

Bourne was deeply influenced also by Twain's contemporary William James, who recommended that Americans work "to rid ourselves of cant and humbug, and to know the truth about ourselves." He spoke these words in addressing the Fifth Annual Meeting of the New England Anti-Imperialist League in 1903. Like Twain, James lamented the rise of "an 'imperialist' party," as he called it, during American intervention in Cuba. It "will command all the crude and barbaric patriotism of the country" and "will be a hard thing to resist," he added, then enumerated the consequences of the war in the Philippines: "the material ruin of the Islands; the transformation of native friendliness to execration; the demoralization of our army, from the war office down—forgery decorated, torture white-washed, massacre condoned; the creation of a chronic anarchy in the Islands, . . . the inoculation of Manila with a floating Yankee scum," all of which had been foretold by people acquainted with the issues.[13] James's litany of imperialist sins resembled later ones chanted by nonviolent activists during subsequent wars of intervention around the globe.

In "The Moral Equivalent of War" (1910), published just before his death, James offered an alternative to the martial spirit then increasing, with sophisticated insights into the psychological necessity of developing nonviolent strategies for social change. Pacifists must do more than preach, he argued; they must act, if they want to divert youthful energies away from warmaking and toward peacemaking. James stressed finding work that satisfies the psychological need associated with heroism in battle —the self-sacrifice, sense of community, and camaraderie characteristic among foot soldiers, even in the bloodiest battle.

Other people who made significant contributions to the philosophy and strategy of nonviolence in this period, building on a tradition of dissent, had little or no knowledge of the tradition of nonviolence before their own time. Early resistance to World War I, for example, depended upon the leadership of those agitating for worker's and women's rights, such as Debs, Berkman, Goldman, and Flynn, rather than upon followers of abolitionists and nonresisters, such as Elihu Burritt or Adin Ballou.

The Socialist Party and the more militant Industrial Workers of the World (IWW) applied the skills they had learned in struggles against child labor and for better working conditions and wages. As young radicals, these anarchists and socialists had advocated acts of violence to bring on "the revolution." After about 1910, however, they shunned this romantic view of initiating social change to bring down "the whole rotten system."

Among various figures who inspired later nonviolent activists and caught the imagination of artists and writers, the most influential were Eugene Victor Debs (1865–1926), five-time nominee for president on the Socialist ticket; William (Big Bill) Haywood (1869–1928), cofounder of the Industrial Workers of the World in 1905; Emma Goldman (1869–1940), a popular speaker and literary essayist; and Elizabeth Gurley Flynn (1890–1962), socialist and later communist organizer and memoirist. The library of poems, novels, and memoirs by and about those figures remain central to the literature of nonviolence.

The young Eugene Victor Debs, who began as a railroad worker and member of the Indiana legislature from Terre Haute, had been radicalized while in jail during the Pullman strike of 1894. Eventually, he inspired a whole generation of people who would make major contributions to the nonviolent tradition. Dorothy Day, cofounder of the Catholic Worker movement in 1933, for example, often referred to Debs's influence upon her life, and reprinted his statement to the judge following his sentencing for draft resistance in 1918:

> While there is a lower class, I am in it; while there is a criminal element,
> I am of it; and while there is a soul in prison, I am not free.

In 1971, Day spoke movingly of Debs, at his gravesite, just before she herself received the annual Debs Award at Indiana State University, Terre Haute.

Debs's famous statement appears also in a lyrical biography of him, "Lover of Mankind," at the very beginning of John Dos Passos's trilogy, *U.S.A.,* and was widely circulated as a handsome poster by Ben Shahn. Ammon Hennacy (1893–1970), Dorothy Day's coworker and fellow anarchist and pacifist, made his way to draft resistance and Christian nonviolence through the influence of Debs and regarded him and Malcolm X as the two greatest figures in American history.

After championing the railroad workers in their struggle for better wages and working conditions, Debs defended men who refused induction during World War I—and indeed remained faithful to the poor and the down and out to the end of his life. As a result of his allegiance to the Socialist Party, he spent extended periods in jail, including the years 1918–21. President Wilson's vindictiveness toward Debs, in refusing him amnesty—after freeing other war resisters at the end of World War I— was one of many reflections of his loyal following.

Debs was already a living legend by the time he went to jail in 1918. A representative account of him, based upon a meeting with two admirers, the journalist John Reed and the artist Art Young, tells of a "tall, shambling, homespun radical with roots in the Greenback Party and Populism, who for twenty years had made socialism seem as American as Thanksgiving . . . a rare combination of courage and humanity. Rising from a sickbed, obviously in pain, Debs welcomed the two visitors with a radiance, affection, and warmth that made him seem a child's version of Uncle Sam. Face glowing, voice intense, he described recent experiences —brushes with vigilantes and detectives, threats of reprisals in small towns."[14]

Debs's method of organizing embodied many of the strategies of nonviolence. He emphasized a personalist approach, much in the manner of Peter Maurin and Ammon Hennacy, and often cautioned those who looked to him for guidance about the dangers of "following the leader":

> I do not want you to follow me or anyone else; if you are looking for a Moses to lead you out of this capitalist wilderness, you will stay right where you are. I would not lead you into the promised land if I could, because if I could lead you in, some one else would lead you out. YOU MUST USE YOUR HEADS AS WELL AS YOUR HANDS, and get yourself out of your present condition.[15]

As with Gandhi, Debs regarded the centralization of power as a principal cause of violence.

Debs and the Socialists advocated draft resistance not out of religious principle but out of loyalty to the workers of the world. In doing so, they subscribed to a principle that was central to the IWW as well and circulated posters and popular pamphlets emphasizing their party's motto, "Don't be a Soldier; be a Man."

As during the Revolutionary and Abolitionist periods, an increase in writings about nonviolence, between 1900 and 1917, reflected the tumultuous, even rebellious times, as significant political minorities—syndicalists, socialists, and anarchists—challenged the dominant political system. Their influence is evident in lively and often handsome periodicals: Debs's *Appeal to Reason,* Goldman's *Mother Earth,* Max Eastman's *Masses,* and *The Liberator;* it is also evident in the nonviolent communities and organizations initiated during this period: anarchist communes and schools, as well as Women's International League for Peace and Freedom (1915), Fellowship of Reconciliation (1915), and American Friends Service Committee (1917).

Another important "learning laboratory" and "training ground" for nonviolence was the Industrial Workers of the World, founded in 1905 by Debs, William (Big Bill) Haywood, Mother Jones, and Lucy Parsons (whose husband was one of the Haymarket "martyrs"). Even more militant than the Socialists, the Wobblies (a nickname of uncertain origin) provided leadership for several major strikes in this period, particularly among previously unorganized migratory workers in lumber and construction camps throughout the West, as well as among unskilled factory workers in the East. Another of their gifts to the nonviolent tradition was the Wobblie balladeer Joe Hill.

Born Joel Hagglund, in Sweden, Joseph Hillstrom (1879–1915) wrote numerous ballads for labor organizing after he joined the IWW local union in San Pedro, California, in 1910. These songs, set to gospel or popular ragtime tunes of the day, appeared in *The Little Red Song Book,* which had gone through forty editions by 1915. Workers carried it in their pockets, using the "education" songs in the manner of the Salvation Army, to preach their message on the street. "If a person can put a few cold, common-sense facts into a song and dress them up in a cloak of humor to take the dryness out of them," Hill argued, "he will succeed in reaching a great number of workers who are too unintelligent or too indifferent to read a pamphlet or an editorial on economic science."[16]

Hill's best known song, "Preacher and the Slave," stated a major theme of his verses, the foolishness of workers hoping for "pie in the sky"; "There is Power in the Union" stated another:

There is pow'r, there is pow'r
In a band of working men,
When they stand hand in hand
There's a pow'r, that's a pow'r
That must rule in every land—
Our Industrial Union Grand.

Arrested on a murder charge, never proved, Hill was executed by the state of Utah in 1915. Elizabeth Gurley Flynn, for whom he wrote "The Rebel Girl" (quoted below), appealed on his behalf to Woodrow Wilson, but unsuccessfully, while the undaunted Hill wrote his last will and testament, ending, "Don't mourn, Organize!" Thousands attended his funeral; he asked, however, that his ashes be strewn throughout the rest of the country, because he "didn't want to be caught dead in Utah." He was later immortalized in "I dreamed I saw Joe Hill last night / Alive as he could be," and was the first of several important folksingers of social protest— Woody Guthrie, Pete Seeger, Phil Ochs, Joan Baez, Utah Phillips, Charlie King. Recognizing the value of song in movements for social change and in keeping the history of those struggles alive, these figures—and lesser known "song writers"—made significant contributions to the literary history of nonviolence as well.

When President Wilson plunged the country into war in April 1917, the Wobblies immediately condemned the war effort in general and conscription in particular. Their position, which appeared in their monthly bulletin, was that

All class conscious members of the Industrial Workers of the World are conscientiously opposed to spilling the life blood of human beings, *not for religious reasons,* as are the Quakers and Friendly Societies, but because we believe that the interests and welfare of the working class in all countries are identical. While we are bitterly opposed to the Imperialist Capitalist Government of Germany, we are against slaughtering and maiming the workers of any country.[17]

Wobblies throughout the world were already suffering "imprisonment, death, and abuse of all kinds" in the struggle for social justice, and they saw no reason to wage a war against their fellow and sister workers abroad. In such statements, they reclaimed the values announced forty years before by Elihu Burritt when he called for "a universal strike against the world war system" in a document signed by tens of thousands of workers in the United States and Western Europe.

Through their activities, as well as their songs, artwork, and organizing, the Wobblies eventually captured the imagination of many well-known writers of the early modernist period (with Dos Passos's *U.S.A.* being, perhaps, the best rendering of that period). Debs, Haywood, and Jones wrote pamphlets and memoirs describing sit-ins in the labor movement and acts of noncooperation, which would be adapted by later activists against injustice and war in the 1930s and 1960s. Dos Passos and Ammon Hennacy greatly admired the Wobblies, and Dorothy Day, arrested with them in Chicago during the First World War, wrote for radical periodicals sympathetic to Wobblies long before she cofounded the *Catholic Worker*.

A turning point for the Wobblies and for the labor movement in general was the Lawrence, Massachusetts, strike of 1912, which exposed the cruelties of "the system," offered alternatives to the violence of the status quo, and dramatized the power of the union. Women working in the huge factories of that manufacturing city, which had one of the highest mortality rates in the country, could not afford to buy the three-dollar dresses they made—much less the fine suits and woolens. In addition, their working conditions were horrible, similar to those of the 145 victims of the infamous Triangle Shirtwaist fire in New York City the year before:

> First a lace of smoke
> decorated the air of the workroom,
> the far wall unfolded
> into fire. The elevator shaft
> spun out flames like a dobbin,
> the last car sank.[18]

At a memorial and protest meeting at the Metropolitan Opera House shortly afterward, Rose Schneiderman, a major organizer, described the characteristic plight of labor in this way: "Every time the workers come out in the only way they know how to protest against conditions which are unbearable, the strong hand of the law is allowed to press down heavily upon us."[19]

In Lawrence, "the strong hand of the law" threatened to crush the workers' revolt of 1912, but with disciplined and persistent nonviolent resistance, workers—speaking numerous foreign languages, but a common language of nonviolence—won the strike. Using a familiar ploy, state troops, with fixed bayonets, had tried, but failed, to provoke workers to violence. "The great unwashed," as the newspapers called the Lawrence workers, sent their children to New York City for safekeeping—a wise tactic that rallied support from journalists and the general public in a parade down Broadway.

James Oppenheim, later editor of *Seven Arts*—a "little magazine" that published the early work of Eugene O'Neill and Robert Frost—captured the spirit of Lawrence in poetry, as Theodore Dreiser and John Dos Passos later did in fiction. Oppenheim took his theme from signs and banners carried by women on the picket line ("We Want Bread and Roses, Too!"), in verses later set to music:

> As we come marching, marching,
>   Unnumbered women dead
> Go crying through our singing
>   Their ancient cry for bread.
> Small art and love and beauty
>   Their drudging spirits knew
> Yes, it is bread we fight for—
>   But we fight for roses, too.

The strength of the labor movement before the First World War is suggested by the humor, and the vigor, of its publications and posters. Representative drawings, frequently reprinted and adapted by later nonviolent "agitators," are Art Young's poster naming the indignities suffered by Jesus and later "workers," and a cartoon in which an army recruiter says of a muscular, headless male figure awaiting an army physical, "At last, the ideal recruit."

"Anarchism and art are in the world for exactly the same kind of reason," Margaret Anderson, editor of the *Little Review,* wrote in 1913.[20] Such doctrines regarding radicalism as "the fine art of the workers" swept through Greenwich Village and similar bohemian centers throughout Europe, though a popular rhyme of the period suggests some people's skepticism about combining aesthetic and social doctrines:

> They draw nude women for the *Masses*
> Thick, fat, ungainly lasses—
> How does that help the working classes?[21]

There is little question, nonetheless, that the combination gave modernist art and literature its bite, its originality, its transforming power. Diverse causes, such as Marxism, anarchism, socialism, industrial unionism, cubism, imagism, futurism, Freudianism, feminism, modernism—all were depicted, expounded, and discussed by talented artists and writers, including James Oppenheim, Eugene O'Neill, Amy Lowell, Upton Sinclair, and Sherwood Anderson in this country, and Bertrand Russell, Romain Rolland, and Pablo Picasso in Europe. Even though some artists were swept up in the First World War, as it and the Red Scare dispersed and undermined social reform, they understood the cultural implications of the war sooner than anyone else.

Emma Goldman's importance to the literary history of nonviolence is most evident in her essays, her many friendships with young artists and activists, and her autobiography, *Living My Life* (1931). Born in Russia, she worked as a seamstress in Rochester, New York, in the 1890s before deciding to give her life to the worker's and women's movements. In the pages of the *Atlantic Monthly,* she wrote enthusiastically about the "new" drama of Ibsen and Strindberg, particularly their dramatizations of the plight of women. Later, she frequented the famous 291 Gallery of Alfred Stieglitz and Georgia O'Keefe, in New York, and inspired others to initiate communities and schools based upon anarchist teachings; both Meridel LeSueur and Muriel Rukeyser, as young women, benefited from these educational experiments.

Through her example and writings, Goldman influenced a number of other well-known writers, including John Reed, author of the first major book on the Russian Revolution, *Ten Days That Shook the World* (1919), following his days as a poet and essayist for *The Masses* and as an organizer of the famous Paterson strike pageant at Madison Square Garden in 1913. Among writers of the next generation, Stanley Kunitz (b. 1905) in "Journal to My Daughter" recalled family members, "a flinty maverick line," setting their table in Worcester, Massachusetts,

> for Maxim Gorky, Emma Goldman,
> and the atheist Ingersoll.[22]

Karl Shapiro (b. 1913) wrote a moving, though at times ironic, tribute, "Death of Emma Goldman," after she died in Canada, in 1940, and a spirited essay acknowledging his sometime-anarchist sentiments.

In 1892, Goldman became involved in the first of many controversies when her lover, Alexander Berkman, left Worcester, Massachusetts, for Homestead, Pennsylvania, to kill Ford Frick, an industrialist who had ordered his hired militia ("goons") to shoot into striking workers. Thereafter, Goldman took to the platform to defend Berkman against attacks by Johann Most and others critical of his action, and she gradually adopted less violent means of instigating social change.

One such effort was the anticonscription league that she initiated during World War I—the principal cause for her being exiled, permanently, to Europe, with Berkman and some 240 other "radicals," during the Red Scare of 1919. This deportation was the brainchild of an ambitious young lawyer named J. Edgar Hoover, scourge of later nonviolent activists and libertarians, including Martin Luther King Jr. and Attorney General, later Senator, Robert Kennedy.

Among memoirists, Elizabeth Gurley Flynn—Wobblie organizer, cofounder of the American Civil Liberties Union, and member of the Communist Party from the late 1920s until her death—contributed much to social reform. Joe Hill, her coworker, conveys something of her spirit in "The Rebel Girl," a song he wrote and set to a ragtime tune shortly before his death in 1915:

> There are women of many descriptions
> In this queer world as everyone knows.
> Some are living in beautiful mansions,
> And wearing the finest of clothes.
> There are blue-blooded queens and princesses,
> All dressed in diamond and pearl.
> But the only and thoroughbred lady
> Is the rebel girl.

Many others acknowledged Flynn's inspiration and example in their later campaigns for justice and peace.

Dorothy Day, after Flynn's release from the Alderson penitentiary, told of hearing her, as a young woman, speaking on behalf of strikers in New York City. "I forsook all prudence," Day wrote, "and emptied my purse, not even leaving myself carfare to get back to the office." Calling attention to the thousands of miners, machinists, and farmers who benefited from Flynn's efforts, Day called Flynn "my sister in the deep sense of the word." As a true member of "the laity," Day continued, Flynn "felt a responsibility to do all in her power in defense of the poor, to protect them against injustice and destitution."[23]

Flynn's autobiography, *I Speak My Piece* (1955), later published as *The Rebel Girl: My First Life, 1906–1926* (1973), is one of the best records of the radical labor movement of that period, indicating the many crossovers between dissent and nonviolence, as well as links in the two traditions regarding philosophy and strategy. Growing up in Concord, New Hampshire, Flynn had read widely, particularly the utopian novels and socialist tracts of Mary Wollstonecraft, Edward Bellamy, and William Morris, and had admired Emma Goldman and Alexander Berkman, whom \she met and eventually followed. As with other activists, she emphasized the importance of building community, a concept important to abolitionism and labor organizing, as well as to Catholic Workers and Plowshares.

Flynn's life dramatizes how issues associated with nonviolence are transferred from one generation to another. Her father had been a member of the Anti-imperialist League during the Spanish-American War; Senator George Hoar of Massachusetts, its founder, had been a prominent abolitionist. Flynn remembered her father reciting a poem by Joaquin Miller about a brutal American general who crushed the independence movement among Filipinos at the time of the war (an incident that prompted Twain's bitter and satiric verses as well). Miller's poem spoke about how "Europe mocks us in our shame" and how "from Maine to far Manila bay the nation bleeds and bows its head." Flynn's Irish father "understood British imperialism, . . . an open window to all imperialism," leading her "to hate unjust wars, which took the land and rights away from other peoples."[24] Gurley Flynn, as many called her, knew through her mother about Susan B. Anthony, Frances Willard, Frederick Douglass, and women's struggle for equal rights, and remained faithful to that tradition by doing "all in her power in defense of the poor to protect them against injustice and destitution," as Day said.

Flynn's autobiographies—she would later write *The Alderson Story: My Life as a Political Prisoner*, about her two and one-half years in Alderson (W.Va.) Federal Women's Reformatory—describe her vast experience as a leader among militant labor organizers throughout the United States. In her books, as in the best writings on nonviolence of this period, Flynn's simple, direct prose tells the story of an emerging counterculture that accounts for much of the resistance to state capitalism in the years since her death.

Through her friendships with Joe Hill and other Wobblies, including her marriage to Carlo Tresca, a handsome Italian anarchist and hero of the Lawrence strike of 1912, Flynn knew firsthand the stories and vivid details of organizing miners and foresters spread over the upper Midwest and vast Rocky Mountain area. She also knew Kate Richards O'Hare, Debs's associate and the principal organizer of the tenant farmers in Oklahoma and Texas. A section of *The Rebel Girl*, "The Children's Crusade," mentions names and describes incidents that have practically disappeared from history—another reason that the alliance between workers and antiwar activists during the period remains relatively unknown. For example, tenant farmers jailed for refusing to participate in World War I were among the last to receive amnesty from President Warren G. Harding in the 1920s.

The roots of workers' opposition to militarism ran deep, as Flynn says in her account of a support gathering for them in New York City, before they carried their war-resistance movement to the houses of Congress in

Washington, D.C. Among many moving accounts about resisters—pacifists by religious and socialist by political conviction—she tells the story of William Madison Hicks, descendant of a famous Quaker, Elias Hicks, who was threatened with lynching before his arrest:

> We heard . . . tales of heart-breaking poverty and labor, chopping cotton, of cruel discrimination by neighbors and townsfolk inflamed by war hysteria and of how these women became tired of petitions to Washington to which there were no answers. Then their "Kate" (i.e. Kate Richards O'Hare) called them to go with her "to see the President."[25]

Eventually, because he could not stand "seeing those kids out there any longer!" President Warren G. Harding gave amnesty to the farmers of the Green Corn Rebellion and released them from Leavenworth (Kans.) Federal Prison.

Such remarkable people provided the background for much of the "politics" of early modernist literature, among the poets and writers coming of age during the First World War. In that period, events as apparently dissimilar as the Paterson, New Jersey, strike and the Armory Art Show, both of which burst upon New York in 1913, informed the lives of artists and social activists alike and overflowed in the writings of John Reed, Upton Sinclair, and the more experimental fiction of John Dos Passos; the poetry of e. e. cummings, William Carlos Williams, and Edna St. Vincent Millay; and the graphic arts of George Bellows and Stuart Davis.

The war ended much of that close association between social activists and artists, as many painters and writers left for Europe in the politically repressive 1920s. The militant unions had been destroyed. In Dos Passos's words, "The rainbowtinted future of reformed democracy went pop like a pricked soapbubble." Only in the 1930s did artists and workers rediscover their common lot and reclaim their earlier, closer, and mutually beneficial association. Then, not surprisingly, the American tradition of nonviolence entered another significant phase of its development.

4

~~~~~~

Draft Resistance and the Labor Movement
1914–1940

A Theory

As Thucydides said,
What is history
Greeks!
Murdering
Greeks

—Thomas McGrath [1]

The beginning of the European war in 1914 coincided with a vital period of social reform and artistic innovation in the United States. By 1905, writers and artists addressed more directly than before the fundamental changes that had shaped and shaken the nation since the Civil War—rapid industrialization, the labor movement, imperial expansion, largescale immigration. In fiction, Upton Sinclair's *Jungle* (1905), the later stories of Mark Twain, and the novels of Theodore Dreiser indicated, by their tone and style, "new directions" associated with public and political discourse; and in *The Promise of American Life* (1909), Herbert Croly, founding editor of the *New Republic*, outlined priorities and programs appropriate to changing economic and social conditions.

Numerous associations and publications initiated over the next five years indicated "new beginnings" in politics and the arts: the National Association for the Advancement of Colored People (1909); the Carnegie Endowment for International Peace (1910); *The Masses* (1911); *Poetry*

(1912); the Armory Art Show (1913); *New Republic* (1914); the Provincetown Players (1915); and, as mentioned earlier, a host of "little magazines" that published the early modernists, including Robert Frost, Amy Lowell, Ezra Pound, William Carlos Williams, Eugene O'Neill, T. S. Eliot, and Marianne Moore.

Trying to imagine "what might have been" had the United States not declared war against the Central Powers in 1917 is rather like trying to imagine "what might have been" had the South succeeded in establishing itself as an independent nation. Such an exercise of the imagination dramatizes, nonetheless, how fundamentally Woodrow Wilson's declaration of war (and the forces unleashed by that decision) undermined movements for social reform already under way in the United States. As with Southerners, people committed to nonviolent social change suffered some hard defeats and learned some hard lessons about the repressive effects of that war from the moment it was declared—and still harder lessons as it continued and after it ended. The change in the cultural climate after 1917 is suggested by an incident in which the government suppressed one journal simply for reprinting Thomas Jefferson's statement encouraging the right to revolution.

Wilson, who had run as "the peace candidate" in 1916, instituted a series of repressive wartime measures threatening free speech and the democratic process soon after the United States entered the war in April 1917. Over the advice and protests of the very moderate American Union Against Militarism, which argued that the ruling undermined people's basic constitutional rights, Congress passed a vaguely defined Espionage Act in June of that year. That law allowed the government to confiscate any literature that caused "insubordination, disloyalty or mutiny" in the military services or that might "embarrass or hamper the Government in conducting the war." Mail was seized, and the following periodicals were censored or suspended: *The Masses* (Max Eastman), *The Appeal to Reason* (Eugene Victor Debs), *The World Tomorrow,* (Norman Thomas), *The Nation* (Oswald Garrison Villard), and the *Michigan Socialist,* the *Milwaukee Leader,* and the *New York Call.* Federal marshalls "corralled radicals of every nationality, faction, and ideological persuasion," and U.S. district attorneys won convictions on charges of treason of labor leaders and antiwar activists.[2] Theodore Roosevelt, among others, recommended shooting German-Americans regarded as disloyal.

Cruelties and injustices during the summer of 1917 included the torture and lynching of Frank Little, a Wobblie antiwar activist in Montana, by local vigilantes, and the beating, burning, and drowning of scores of African Americans in East St. Louis, Illinois. In Bisbee, Arizona, local patriots cooperated with state officials in loading 1,200 Wobblie miners in cattle cars and deporting them, with limited provisions, to the New Mexico desert. As late as 1919, after the war ended, sixty-two men and women were publicly identified as having been under surveillance. That list, a kind of "who's who" of pacifism or radicalism, included Norman Thomas, John Haynes Holmes, John Nevin Sayre, Jane Addams, Emily Greene Balch, Elizabeth Gurley Flynn, Charles A. Beard, Scott Nearing, and Rufus M. Jones—many of whom had been important to organizations for social change for decades.

An important focus for "nonviolent alternatives" during the war was provided by Debs's Socialist Party and the Industrial Workers of the World, as well as by individual anarchists such as Emma Goldman and Alexander Berkman, who organized an anticonscription league. The consequences of their nonviolent resistance were serious: Debs served three years in Atlanta Federal Prison for encouraging, then standing with, young socialists who refused induction; Kate Richards O'Hare and other socialists and Wobblies spent time in jail; and Goldman and Berkman were subsequently deported to Europe, vigorously pursued by J. Edgar Hoover.

Such war hysteria led to the harassment and persecution of German Americans, including the novelist Theodore Dreiser. H. L. Mencken, at the height of his career as essayist and social critic, came to Dreiser's defense; but writers and artists, with the exception of Randolph Bourne and a few others, endorsed or tolerated Wilson's policies regarding war and conscription, once they were imposed in 1917.

In England, even in the midst of strong patriotic sentiment, well-known writers and artists had openly befriended and supported young conscientious objectors to war. Lytton Strachey and Virginia and Leonard Woolf, for example, welcomed them at Garsington Manor, near Oxford, the residence/retreat of Lady Ottoline Morrell. Bertrand Russell spoke out vigorously against the government's declaration of war, eventually losing his Cambridge University fellowship for doing so. Siegfried Sassoon, after befriending his young compatriot and fellow officer Wilfred Owen (while both recovered from shell shock at Craiglockhart Hospital in Scotland in 1917), risked arrest and possible imprisonment for speaking out against war propaganda and the slaughter on the western front.

Younger writers in the United States who later dominated the literary scene, meanwhile, went enthusiastically to what some of them regarded as "a great adventure" in Europe. Like Frederick Henry, in Hemingway's *Farewell to Arms* (1929)—and the author himself—e. e. cummings, Malcolm Cowley, and John Dos Passos joined the ambulance corps and William Faulkner journeyed to Canada to sign up, before the United States declared war against Germany.

Later, Hemingway, Faulkner, Dos Passos, and cummings all wrote indictments of war that were much more devastating, in fact, than those by committed pacifists. Their novels and stories, together with major poems of Ezra Pound and T. S. Eliot, who lived in England during the war, and Willa Cather's novel *One of Ours* (1922), contributed to the pacifist movement during the 1930s and had a lasting effect on public attitudes toward modern warfare, as Paul Fussell and other literary historians have suggested. Antiwar statements by the early modernists—Edna St. Vincent Millay's poem "Conscientious Objection" is representative— were vigorous, even militant, but only after the fact, not while the war was going on.

Wartime repression had merely confirmed the fears of Addams, Debs, Goldman, and others who had opposed America's entrance from the beginning. At that time, the case against U.S. participation found its most insightful, eloquent voice, however, in Randolph Bourne (1886–1918), a literary and social critic who had witnessed the coming of the war in Europe as a Watson Fellow in 1913–1914 and had returned home to become the first education editor for the *New Republic*.

A disciple of John Dewey and author of *The Gary Schools* (1916), Bourne regarded Wilson's arguments for war as thinly disguised British propaganda and, worse, as the rhetoric of "the State," which "speciously rational" intellectuals, including Dewey, appropriated uncritically. Bourne's charges strongly resembled those made against intellectuals, during the Vietnam War and afterward, who "identified themselves with the least democratic forces in American life. . . . They have assumed the leadership for war of those very classes whom the American democracy has been immemorially fighting," rather than "endeavoring to clear the public mind of the cant of war, to get rid of old mystical notions that clog our thinking."[3]

In an argument with his former mentor in the pages of the *New Republic*, Bourne scrutinized John Dewey's easy justifications for violence, and was eventually ostracized by editors and harassed by police as a result of his unpopular stand. Because of his criticism of U.S. policy in essays later published as *The Untimely Papers* (1919), a nervous patron discontinued funding for *The Seven Arts*, the most sophisticated of the early modernist "little magazines." Edited by James Oppenheim, the author of "Bread and Roses," *The Seven Arts* published Bourne's essays beside the early poems of Robert Frost and others who would dominate the American literary scene in the 1920s.

Bourne's arguments against active U.S. participation in the Great War were political rather than moral or religious. Though not a pacifist, his rationale reflected the influence of Tolstoy's criticism of the state as well as that of antiimperialists such as Twain and William James a generation before, even as it anticipated later nonviolent resisters and strategists. As early as 1914, Bourne understood the various links in the chain of what he called "social consciousness": feminism, socialism, social religion, internationalism. He was exploring something that Gandhi began to explore about the same time in resisting British rule in India: the power of nonviolence in mediation and reconciliation. Bourne thought the United States could use its influence more effectively as arbitrator or mediator than as combatant to bring the Allies and the Central Powers to the conference table and to peace. As a participant, the United States only extended the military campaign and further complicated any political settlement, he argued.

In "Who Owns the Universities?" (1915), Bourne defended Scott Nearing, economist and political radical, after his being fired from the University of Pennsylvania; and in "Those Columbia Trustees" (1917), Bourne came to the aid of James McKeen Cattell and Henry Wadsworth Longfellow Dana after they were fired by that university, saying that "Professor Dana's only offense was that he retained his pacific and internationalist philosophy in wartime, and associated with other radicals who had retained theirs."[4] Bourne's attack on the university for its complicity with right-wing ideologies is echoed by later critics of the academy in wartime. His "War and the Intellectuals" is the first social critique of its kind, in a literary line running from the First World War to the present, including among others Paul Goodman's "Causerie Against the Military Industrial Complex" (1969) and Noam Chomsky's *American Power and the New Mandarins* (1969).

Bourne regarded the war as "immoral" and as a "bad strategy," as he said in "Conscience and Intelligence in War":

> Not all the pacifist feeling has had an evangelical color. There is an element of antiwar sentiment which has tried to be realistic, and does not hope to defeat war merely by not doing something. Though events have been manipulated against it, this element neither welcomes martyrdom nor hopes to be saved for its amiable sentiments.[5]

The strength of Bourne's position arises from his psychological insight into the tendency of wartime thinking to ignore everything but victory or total victory. In such an atmosphere, any challenge to the war mentality that promises to be effective is automatically crushed "under even the most democratic governments." Further, the fact that "war blots out the choice of ends and even of means should be the final argument against its use as a technique for any purpose whatever."

On the basis of his reputation as a social and literary critic (he died in the influenza epidemic shortly after the armistice in 1918), Bourne emerged as a kind of patron saint among artists who recognized the folly of Wilson's "war to end war." Bourne's writings have been cited by successive generations of social critics, who hold conformist intellectuals and jingoist academics responsible for the state's abuse of power and the culture's attendant moral decline.

For that reason, and for his autobiographical essay, "An American Literary Radical," published posthumously in Scofield Thayer's influential *Dial* magazine, Bourne occupies a significant place in the nonviolent tradition. Thayer had intended Bourne to be the political editor of *The Dial*, which published the best in modernist writing that explored the full psychological and philosophical implications of the war, such as Eliot's *Waste Land* (1922).

In many ways, Bourne's writings anticipated in subject matter and tone the writings of poets and novelists who focused on the religious and philosophical implications of "the senseless slaughter," as Hemingway called it. Bourne's portraits of young conscripts during the war resemble the fictional characters in works by the "lost generation" of the 1920s, the young men in John Dos Passos's *One Man's Initiation* (1919) and *Three Soldiers* (1921), for example, and in Hemingway's *Sun Also Rises* (1926). Bourne's language and tone suggest, as well, Wilfred Owen's ironic antiwar poems ("Futility" and "Dulce et Decorum Est") and Ezra Pound's devastating lyrics about battles on the western front, where young men "walked eye-deep in hell / believing in old men's lies." Lines from *Hugh Selwyn Mauberley* (1919) tell of the "myriad" who died

> For an old bitch gone in the teeth
> For a botched civilization . . .
> For two gross of broken statues,
> For a few thousand battered books.

No one described the war's consequences and the accompanying decline of Western civilization more succinctly, more accurately, than Pound, a full decade before the existentialists called for a full "revaluation of values." As with other activists and artists, Pound never quite reclaimed the optimism and enthusiasm that characterized his earlier work—the same hope and energy that belonged, as Bourne's did, to the prewar period.

In resisting and exposing the rhetoric of war, Bourne joined radical labor organizers, socialists, and anarchists of the period in confronting issues that haunt the modern warmaking state. His insights into the modern dilemma, the alienation and depersonalization associated with technology and bureaucracy, were the ones that gave early modernism its "sting" and that remained central to the literary and graphic arts, once the war ended.

In his challenging and exposing facile or intellectually pretentious justifications for war, Bourne—and his friend Van Wyck Brooks, to a lesser degree—fulfilled his responsibility as a critic of "imperial" America much in the manner that Tolstoy did for "imperial" Russia and that several members of the Bloomsbury group, including E. M. Forster, Bertrand Russell, and Virginia Woolf, did for "imperial" England. As the cultural historian Martin Green has indicated, critics of imperialism—and the counterculture associated with them—have accompanied movements for nonviolent social change over the past two centuries. In developing this thesis with great skill, Green focused initially, in *Children of the Sun* (1976), on English writers and aesthetes in the 1920s; this book was followed by comparative biographies of Tolstoy and Gandhi and commentaries on the Armory Art Show and the Paterson strike in the United States in 1913, both of which were important to Bourne.

Thus he has remained an important reference point for nonviolent activists since his untimely death at thirty-three in 1918, and activists and writers still regard him as a standard against which they measure intellectuals in any age. For example, the Catholic Worker Ammon Hennacy, arrested thirty-two times for resisting the draft, nuclear weapons, and capital punishment, often told the story of how he gave up his bed to Bourne when Bourne traveled from New York to speak at the University of Wisconsin, Madison, in 1915; and Hennacy frequently quoted Bourne with admiration in his leaflets and books. Dorothy Day, who wrote for *The Masses* about the same time as Bourne, quoted his famous epigram, "War is the health of the state," in the pages of *The Catholic Worker*. Writers as varied as Theodore Dreiser, John Dos Passos, Robert Bly, and Noam Chomsky have regarded Bourne as a prophetic figure who understood the psychological and political consequences of total war; and he is still frequently cited in imaginative and polemical writings associated with nonviolence.

Equally important to the history of nonviolence after 1915 were the efforts made by, and minor successes of, traditional peace churches in winning official recognition and approval for alternate service for young men who, on religious grounds, refused to go to war. Several young men, including Richard L. Stierhiem, distinguished themselves in battle, even as they adamantly resisted shooting a gun. Drafted and sent overseas long before the government officially recognized conscientious objection, Stierhiem refused to serve and deserted his unit; arrested, he was court-martialed, convicted, and sentenced to death. Awaiting execution, he volunteered to go into No Man's Land—the space between the trenches, where as many as eighty thousand had died in a single campaign—and, unassisted, rescued six wounded men under machine-gun fire; later, he buried the dead, exposing himself all the while to imminent death. Some-time later, he was assigned to noncombatant service upon the recommendation of General John J. Pershing.

In addition to similar tales, novelists and poets of the 1920s wrote exposés of the bureaucratic war machine, such as e. e. cumming's moving memoir, *The Enormous Room* (1922). An autobiographical narrative, it tells about cummings and his compatriot in the American ambulance corps, who were mistaken for spies in France and were eventually arrested and imprisoned on charges of treason. Cumming's protest—languid, whimsical, "beat"—is quite apolitical toward events surrounding the war; it is an individualistic, sarcastic gesture, ridiculing the confusion and mind-lessness of petty bureaucrats who do the government's work. Cummings, his compatriot, and their eccentric fellow prisoners—including a count, a gypsy, a clown, and a giant—maintain a kind of nutty, persistent human-ity during their captivity, in spite of the filth of the place and the cruelty of the guards.

As prison literature, *The Enormous Room* bears some resemblance to later, more politically sophisticated wartime memoirs—Jack Cook's *Rags of Time* (1972), for example, from the Vietnam period. Always the indi-vidualist, cummings—cranky and irascible rather than reformist, more anachronist than anarchist—seldom extends his critique to the social order. As a tour de force, his memoir complements, nonetheless, the testimony of activists jailed for conscience's sake in the same period—Debs, Berkman, Goldman, Flynn, and Hennacy.

More important to the nonviolent tradition in literature, perhaps, is cummings's later poetic tribute to individual, principled resistance, "I Sing of Olaf" (1931). Kicked and cursed by his officers, "a yearning nation's blueyed pride," and beaten by his fellow soldiers, Olaf refused to knuckle under: "I will not kiss your f.ing flag . . . there is some s. I will not eat." Meanwhile, in the hallowed halls of Washington, D.C.,

> our president, being of which
> assertions duly notified
> threw the yellowsonofbitch
> into a dungeon, where he died

In a prayer for mercy, the speaker recognizes Olaf as a hero, a secular saint,

> preponderatingly because
> unless statistics lie he was
> more brave than me; more blond than you.

A vivid and sympathetic portrait of a conscientious objector "whose warmest heart recoiled at war," cummings's poem was widely reprinted and recited at rallies against the Indochina war (cummings's widow, however, would not allow it to be included in Robert Bly and David Ray's anthology, *A Poetry Reading Against the Vietnam War* [1966], perhaps because of cummings's conservative political views).

Although the author himself took a conventionally "macho," even aggressive, stance toward conflict and relationships with others, Ernest Hemingway wrote, nonetheless, the most powerful antiwar novel in literature. Frederick Henry, the central character of *A Farewell to Arms,* goes to Italy to serve in the ambulance corps believing in the Allied cause, much as Hemingway did. Living and fighting among Italian peasants after he is practically blown to pieces while eating a piece of cheese, Henry falls in love with a beautiful young English nurse, Catherine Barkeley, whose fiancé had previously died in the war. Her regret that they never made love before he died contributes, in some ways, to her "availability" as Henry's lover, though she has no illusions about his romantic ardor.

As a result of his experiences at the front and in a narrow escape among Italian troops in mutiny, Henry bids "a farewell to arms" and escapes to Switzerland with Catherine, where she soon dies in childbirth. At the end, with his love and their baby dead, Henry walks out of the hospital and into the rain and a world whose Messiah, according to an earlier passage, remains indifferent toward and perhaps even delights in the suffering of His creations. In this passage, as with Bourne's antiwar essays, the ironic later stories of Mark Twain are undoubtedly an influence.

As a statement about war, *A Farewell to Arms* remains, after more than sixty years, one of the most accurate renderings of war, including those victimized long after the last shot was fired. Although the novel, as with others about the First World War, seldom suggests what peace might be like, it provides a powerful warning about the consequences of "total war." Millions die in combat; millions more are permanently maimed, physically, psychologically, spiritually.

Erich Maria Remarque's *All Quiet on the Western Front* (1929), later a popular and critically-acclaimed film, and Robert Graves's *Goodbye to All That* (1929) contributed to the strong antiwar sentiment of the 1930s (and contributed to the antiwar movement among students of the 1960s). Two other American novels, *Company K* (1933) by William March, which was influential among writers, and *Johnny Got His Gun* (1939) by Dalton Trumbo, which was immensely popular as a book and a film, excoriated the waste and cruelty of modern war, in a manner resembling Wilfred Owen's poems.

As these works appeared, the writings and example of Mohandas Gandhi were also beginning to attract the attention of readers and activists in the United States, particularly among African Americans. Both W. E. B. Du Bois, scholar and cofounder of the NAACP, and Marcus Garvey, leader of "the largest and most dramatic black mass movement ever to exist in America," quoted Gandhi in their writings and speeches and emphasized the "ideological, historical, and personal links between the Indian struggle for independence and the African-American freedom movement."[6] Du Bois, as editor of the NAACP publication, *The Crisis,* invited Gandhi to contribute to its twentieth-anniversary issue. His remarks in "To the American Negro" (July 1929 issue), widely reprinted, strengthened the bond between African Americans working for social justice in the United States and Indian nationals working for home rule; they also helped to prepare the way, as one historian has said, for "a Black Gandhi" in this country, that is, Martin Luther King Jr.

In 1929, also, Charles Freer Andrews—an Anglican missionary associated with Gandhi in South Africa and India—brought the Mahatma's message to the United States. The following year, *The Power of Nonviolence* by Richard B. Gregg, a Quaker, extended Gandhi's message of nonviolence that is still central to understanding the concept. And in 1935, a delegation of African Americans, including Howard Thurman, chaplain of Howard University, journeyed to India to visit not only with Gandhi, but also with Rabindranath Tagore, Nobel laureate, poet, and advocate of nonviolent direct action. After being assured by Thurman "that African-Americans were ready to receive the message of nonviolence," Gandhi said, somewhat prophetically, that it "may be through the Negroes that the unadulterated message of nonviolence will be delivered to the world";[7] two decades later, through the Civil Rights movement, it was.

A significant nonviolent campaign involving well-known writers in the latter 1920s was the struggle to defend Nicola Sacco (1891–1927) and Bartolomeo Vanzetti (1888–1927). The fish peddler and the eloquent shoemaker were charged with robbery and murder and were executed by the state of Massachusetts in 1927 (to be pardoned by the state, ironically, in 1976). Edna St. Vincent Millay and Katherine Anne Porter, who participated in demonstrations at the federal courthouse in Boston, and John Dos Passos, who was eventually arrested in the campaign, all wrote works about this tragic miscarriage of justice, another consequence of the Red Scare that sent Goldman and Berkman out of the country in 1919 and essentially destroyed the labor movement until its revival during the 1930s.

The Sacco and Vanzetti trial has been credited with bringing expatriate writers home and with encouraging them to address and to commit themselves to needed social change in the United States. Writers returned and went to work, in spite of the fact that many of them regarded their native country much as did Scofield Thayer, editor of the brilliant "little magazine," *The Dial;* he could not publish sections of *Ulysses,* he wrote to James Joyce, because "we in America live and move and have our being in the sinister shadow of an appallingly Presbyterian post office." By 1930, writers had begun to identify with the plight of workers and the down and out, as they had before the war—a change reflected in the tone and attitude of literature during the Great Depression.

Although generally regarded as a social rather than a literary movement, the Catholic Worker movement has contributed significantly to all aspects of the nonviolent tradition, including the literary, with fiction, nonfiction, poetry, and drama. Beginning as a four-page newspaper, with 2,500 copies distributed among a 1933 May Day crowd at Union Square, New York City, the movement was founded by Peter Maurin, a French peasant and itinerant worker and teacher, and Dorothy Day, an American journalist and radical. *The Catholic Worker* became a monthly newspaper and still sells at a penny a copy. It is to the American tradition of nonviolence what the *Massachusetts Spy* was to the movement for independence or what Garrison's *Liberator* was to the movement for abolition. Before the *Worker* was published, Tolstoy's Christian nonviolence informed the minds and hearts of many Americans; but with publication of the *Worker* on May 1, 1933 (heavily indebted to Maurin's "Easy Essays"), the word became flesh. Neither the United States nor the Catholic Church—nor, indeed, the nonviolent tradition—has ever been quite the same since.

On the fortieth anniversary of its founding, Dwight MacDonald, writing in *The New Yorker,* said that *The Catholic Worker* newspaper "hit Union Square with an ambiguous thud. The Marxian native couldn't classify this political chimera: its fore quarters were anarchistic but its hinder parts were attached to the Church of Rome."[8] Although she rightly regarded Peter Maurin as her teacher because his ideas and example provoked her to action, Dorothy Day is regarded as central to the movement's literary history, in light of her close friendships with radical journalists,

Marxist critics, and with playwrights, novelists, and poets (Michael Gold, Eugene O'Neill, Caroline Gordon, Malcolm Cowley, and Allen Tate).

Born in Brooklyn in 1897, Dorothy Day, whose father was also a journalist, had grown up in Chicago and attended the University of Illinois, on scholarship. There, she became a socialist and soon headed for New York. A convert to Catholicism in 1926, Day had been well schooled in the American radical tradition through her reading and personal associations. She had been jailed with Wobblies and feminists just before World War I, had worked as a secretary for Floyd Dell and written for his magazine, *The Masses,* and had been a friend of Eugene O'Neill, Allen Tate, and other well-known writers of the period.

Day had converted to Catholicism after reading *The Varieties of Religious Experience* (1902), by that enduring though not always visible "presence" in the nonviolent tradition, William James. Day greatly admired Eugene Victor Debs and wanted most to follow in the footsteps of Emma Goldman and Elizabeth Gurley Flynn. In addition to her own achievements as novelist, screenwriter, journalist, editor, and memoirist, Day attracted a host of other writers and artists to the movement, some as active participants, among whom were Ade Bethune, J. F. Powers, John Cogley, Michael Harrington, William Everson (Brother Antoninus), Thomas Merton, and Daniel Berrigan, and some as "fellow travelers" and benefactors, among whom were W. H. Auden, Fritz Eichenberg, Gordon Zahn, Robert Coles, Jack Cook, and Charlie King. All have contributed to the Catholic Worker movement.

In the literature of nonviolence, Dorothy Day's writings occupy a special place in argument and style. Although the publication of her first novel enabled her to work briefly as a scriptwriter in Hollywood in the 1920s, Day was primarily an essayist and memoirist, and the persistence (one hesitates to call it "success") of the movement owes much to her skill as a storyteller. Repeatedly, with simplicity, yet assurance and clarity, she retold the story of her initial meeting with Peter Maurin; her giving up of her common-law husband, Foster Batterham, in order to rear their daughter, Tamar, as a Catholic; and her journeys "On Pilgrimage"—the title of her monthly column—to visit Houses of Hospitality that feed the poor and house the homeless, throughout this country. On these journeys, she traveled by bus or drove dilapidated cars, wearing the clothes others had donated to the Catholic Worker. With only her religious faith and community to sustain her, Day and her associates performed—and those surviving her still perform—the daily works of mercy, attending to the down and out whom nobody else cared for or wanted, while resisting injustice, the draft, and nuclear armaments on the street or in jail.

As with earlier pacifists, from William Penn to Gandhi, the Catholic

Worker movement emphasizes not only active witness against injustice but also the building of community. Sixty years after its founding, one can point to the rich legacy of over one hundred farms and Houses of Hospitality, from New York to Hawaii, from Minnesota to Texas, and in Australia, the Netherlands, and England. The movement has also published countless newspapers—modest, but often handsome, with the drawings of Fritz Eichenberg, Rita Corbin, and Ade Bethune. As Day wrote in the conclusion of *The Long Loneliness* (1952), the story of her conversion (which also appeared, fittingly, on a remembrance card at the time of her death in 1980): "We have all known the long loneliness and we have learned that the only solution is love and that love comes with community."

In justifying her resistance to "the whole rotten system," Dorothy Day usually cited European writers such as Dickens and Dostoevsky, as well as Ignazio Silone and George Orwell. The literary enthusiasms of her associate Ammon Hennacy, on the other hand, were the writings of anarchists and socialists, especially Tolstoy and Kropotkin, though he committed many poems to memory, including several by William Blake, as well the songs of Joe Hill and other Wobblie balladeers.

Although Day regarded Hennacy as "contentious" and regretted his satiric remarks about the church she loved, she acknowledged his influence on the Catholic Worker movement and admired his courage, particularly his initiating civil disobedience against nuclear air-raid drills in New York City in the 1950s. In a moving preface to *The Autobiography of a Catholic Anarchist* (1955), she said that the story of Hennacy's imprisonment in Atlanta as a draft resister during World War I ranks "with the great writings of the world about prison."[9]

Thrown in "the hole," during his confinement, after leading a strike against the rotten fish being served to the prisoners, Hennacy contemplated suicide. He had actually sharpened a spoon in order to cut his wrists, when the sight of Alexander Berkman, "with the fighting spirit that jails could not kill," restored his determination not "to chicken," as he put it:

> Tears came into my eyes and I felt ashamed of myself for my cowardly idea of suicide just because I had a few reverses. Here was Berkman who had passed through much more than I would ever have to endure if I stayed two more years in solitary.[10]

Determined to show his persecutors that he would be a credit to his ideals, Hennacy recited from memory Edwin Markham's "The Man with the

Hoe" to keep up his spirit, then "sang cheerfully" the last verses of the IWW Prison Song:

> By all the graves of Labor's dead,
> By Labor's deathless flag of red,
> We make a solemn vow to you,
> We'll keep the faith, we will be true.

Released from prison in the early 1920s, he worked as a common laborer most of his life, refusing all along to pay taxes or to file an income tax form on behalf of "the war-making State."

The Book of Ammon (1965), a revised and expanded version of *Autobiography of a Catholic Anarchist,* gives the full, moving, and lively account of Hennacy's eventual conversion from socialism to Christian anarchism and nonviolence. His posthumously published *The One Man Revolution in America* (1970), to which this book is indebted, describes the tradition that sustained him during thirty-two arrests and long periods in jail: Paine, Jefferson, Garrison, Debs, Day, and Malcolm X, among others. The example of the Hopi Indians, among whom Hennacy lived and worked during the 1940s and 1950s, dramatized for him the contributions of the Native American tradition to nonviolence.

For many who knew him, Hennacy remains the model activist, "a real radical," as J. F. Powers, novelist and short story writer who was imprisoned for draft resistance during World War II, has said. Sustained by his wit, his courage, and his close association with working people, Hennacy remained high-spirited, persistent, witty in or out of jail, through years of begging for food to serve at Catholic Worker Houses of Hospitality, including Joe Hill House, in Salt Lake City. An inveterate talker and teacher, he advocated a diet of "no fish, flesh, or fowl," and singled-mindedly, often joyously, encouraged others to disagree with his "non-church Christian anarchism."

In summarizing his "Radical Philosophy," Hennacy could be poetic about his wayward native country, which he refused to desert "to those who would bring it to atomic ruin," for

> Truly America the Beautiful means much to me. . . . Despite the two warmongering Roosevelts and Wilson, I think of Altgeld, old Bob La-Follette and Debs. Despite the Klan and Legion vigilantes, I think of the old-time Wobblies, of Sacco and Vanzetti, and of Berkman and Emma Goldman. Despite the warmongering churches I think of the old-time Quakers who paid no taxes for war and who hid escaped slaves.[11]

His most famous saying, however, written after a day's work in the field in 1945, is a brief credo of nonviolence:

> Love without courage and wisdom is sentimentality, as with the ordinary church member. Courage without love and wisdom is foolhardiness, as with the ordinary soldier. Wisdom without love and courage is cowardice, as with the ordinary intellectual. Therefore one who has love, courage, and wisdom is one in a million who moves the world, as with Jesus, Buddha and Gandhi.[12]

The Catholic Worker movement was only one of many positive, communal efforts to heal "the invisible scar" of the 1930s, an important decade for nonviolence because workers who resisted injustice and initiated social change also altered, indirectly, the course of American art and literature. In 1933, thirty-seven peace organizations formed a National Peace Conference, as the Fellowship of Reconciliation, Women's International League for Peace and Freedom, War Resister's League, and traditional peace churches strengthened a commitment to nonviolence among young people soon to face a difficult moral decision about going to war. Central figures in the larger effort for peace reform included Jessie Wallace Haughan, Norman Thomas, A. J. Muste, and Reinhold Niebuhr, though this popular and influential theologian eventually criticized the pacifist position.[13]

It became virtually impossible for serious writers to avert their eyes from harsh realities, as Daniel Aaron has said, because they provided "topics of greater magnitude for literature than the private and nonpolitical dilemmas of sensitive individualists." Although no single artist conveyed the full sweep of the Great Depression with a "Balzacian grasp of its details" or a "Tolstoyan insight to comprehend its social turbulence,"[14] Dos Passos's trilogy, *U.S.A.* (1936), provided the best chronicle of events leading up to the decade. Dos Passos, along with Dreiser, Hemingway, and other major writers, also published excellent articles on the plight of the poor and the down and out; and several novels, including *The Disinherited* (1933) by Jack Conroy and *In Dubious Battle* (1926) and *The Grapes of Wrath* (1939) by John Steinbeck, successfully dramatized workers' efforts to win decent wages and working conditions.

Among Muriel Rukeyser's early and most effective poems, "The Disease" recounts a miner's conversation with and questions to a doctor, who is explaining the "progress" of silocosis:

It gradually chokes off the air cells in the lungs?
I am trying to say it the best I can.
That is what happens, isn't it?
A choking-off in the air cells?
Yes.
There is difficulty in breathing.
Yes.
And a painful cough?
Yes.
Does silicosis cause death?
Yes.[15]

The alliance between artist and victim, reflected in Rukeyser's poem, led quite naturally to her poems about others "in struggle," from the Scottsboro boys in Alabama and loyalists defending the republic in Spain in the 1930s, to women trying to free themselves from male domination in the 1950s and 1960s, to foreign poets imprisoned in South Korea and others victimized by cold war in the 1970s (discussed in chap. 6).

A telling moment for workers and nonviolence in the 1930s, "the radical decade," was a United Auto Workers (UAW) strike at Fisher Body No. 1, in Flint, Michigan, in late 1936. Refusing to be dislodged from their factory, the strikers settled in for the night—for many nights—unfurled banners, and sang:

When the speed-up comes, just twiddle your thumbs,
    Sit-down! Sit-down!
When the boss won't talk, don't take a walk,
    Sit-down! Sit-down!

The UAW, associated with the new Committee for Industrial Organization, had borrowed the "sit-down" strategy from the French. Refusing to move, yet restraining anyone from harming the plant, fifteen hundred men lived in the factory for over a month. In a telegram to the governor, who eventually sided with them, the workers warned that "the introduction of the militia, sheriffs, or police with murderous weapons will mean a blood-bath of unarmed workers. . . . We fully expect that if a violent effort to oust us is made many of us will be killed, and we take this means of making it known to our wives, our children, to the people of the state of Michigan and the country that if this result follows from the attempt to eject us, you are the one who must be held responsible for our deaths."[16]

Among writers who have focused on these dramatic events, including successes such as the Flint strike, Meridel LeSueur (b. 1900), a longtime activist from the Midwest, has shown a particular sensitivity to the implications of nonviolent struggle. "Born at the beginning of the swiftest and bloodiest century," she herself has been arrested for civil disobedience, most recently in connection with the Honeywell Project, named for the manufacturer of "command systems" for nuclear weapons. LeSueur carries the nonviolent tradition in her bones, as she suggested in speaking of her ancestors', "being preachers, abolitionists, agrarians, radical lawyers on the Lincoln, Illinois circuit. Dissenters and democrats and radicals through five generations."

LeSueur's stories, published in *The Dial* during the 1920s and in *Kenyon Review* during the 1930s, reflected the impact of the Sacco and Vanzetti trial and the suffering of those who risked everything for better wages and working conditions. In "Corn Village" (1930), one of her earliest and best stories, she discusses, with particular insight, the Midwestern/Southwestern roots of "resistance" and Debsian socialism:

> Like many Americans I will never recover from my sparse childhood in Kansas. The blackness, weight, and terror of childhood in mid-America strike deep into the stem of life. Like desert flowers we learned to crouch near the earth, fearful that we would die before the rains, cunning, waiting the season of good growth.[17]

LeSueur's ability to convey the stark realities of the plains gives her work, as it did Willa Cather's, its particular strength.

Working in Kansas and the Dakotas during the early 1930s, LeSueur began making notes about how women "suffered, how we were destroyed, macerated, ground out—and my pockets were full of these notes to the world, this cry from the belly." In her stories, she juxtaposes physical hunger and spiritual abundance, economic poverty and fertile landscapes, much in the manner of Woody Guthrie, the wandering balladeer from Oklahoma, whose songs belong to the same period. Although many of LeSueur's characters—mothers, workers, alienated intellectuals—are defeated by violent circumstance (the Sacco and Vanzetti executions or the Ludlow, Colorado, massacre), others move through hardship, by way of nonviolent direct action, to momentary triumphs.

In her personal example as well as in her best-known stories, LeSueur conveys the history of people sustained by a past one usually hears about only in regional histories or personal memoirs. What in other "proletarian" literature in the 1930s was often merely rhetorical becomes, in her "I Was Marching," for example, concrete and vivid. Set in the Minneapolis trucker's strike of 1937, it is about a young woman who learns the joy of cooperation and resistance. In "Annunciation," another woman, pregnant and hungry, regards the blossoming pear tree outside her window as a promise of better days. One might say of LeSueur's women what Steinbeck implies of Ma Joad, the mother who keeps the family together in *The Grapes of Wrath,* or what Faulkner says of Dilsey, the older black woman who cares for the Compson family in *The Sound and the Fury:* "they endure."

By background and experience, LeSueur was a true daughter of the pre-World War I labor wing of the nonviolent tradition. Her mother chaired the English department at People's College, founded by Eugene Victor Debs and Helen Keller, in South Central Kansas; and LeSueur, studying at the Academy of Dramatic Arts in New York, lived in one of Emma Goldman's anarchist communes before writing for the *New Masses* and other political magazines.

These experiences prepared LeSueur to address issues of justice and peace not as a preacher—someone with the right opinions—but as an artist who described with authority the harsh reality and quiet strength of workers' lives. She was aware not only of the obvious weakness and cruelties of the system but also of the hidden strengths that allowed for movement, new beginnings, and new directions. Her literary art resembles the photographic art of Dorothea Lange in this period, whose "Migrant Mother," for example, caught the persistence as well as the discouragement of a family victimized by the depression. As with other "radicals," LeSueur's work remained somewhat under a cloud, until the women's movement revived interest in it in the 1970s and led to the republication of her best stories and novels, including a one-act play based upon her story "The Girl," in the 1980s.

A poet frequently associated with LeSueur, though he belongs to the next generation, is Thomas McGrath (1914–1989), who evokes the promise of social change during the depression years. His poem of epic length, *Letter to an Imaginary Friend* (1962, 1970), while centered in a later period of war resistance and social agitation, dramatizes the powerful link between the spirit of the 1930s and of the 1960s. That spirit inspired his poems, as it did those of his contemporary, Muriel Rukeyser. Both associated resistance and renewal with the power of poetry, which McGrath once described as "primarily an apparatus, a machine, a plant, a flower, for the creation of real consciousness." In maintaining and deepening the spirit of the 1930s through his work in the 1960s, 1970s, and 1980s, McGrath waged his own nonviolent struggle against a "false consciousness," that is, "the continual present" that robs Americans of a more humane past, a better future. Through his poetry, as E. P. Thompson

(1924–1993), English historian and director of Europe's Campaign for Nuclear Disarmament, said, McGrath's "poetry refuses to permit time to cancel experience like a used stamp"; it resurrects "an alternative present" as a way of allowing for an alternative future.[18]

Although he remained ambivalent personally about nonviolence as a means of social change, many of McGrath's poems convey the values associated with that method and strategy. Like LeSueur, he identified his commitment to social change with life on the Great Plains, "between the Mississippi and the Rocky Mountains, the unmapped country" where "what was real, in all that unreal talk . . . was the generous wish," as the narrator says in the conclusion to *Letter to an Imaginary Friend,* Book I:

> To talk of the People
> Is to be a fool. But they were the *sign* of the People,
> Those talkers. . . .
> A dream surely. Sentimental with its
> Concern for injustice (which no one admits can exist). . . .
>
> And it's all there somewhere.
>   Under the hornacle mine . . .
> In the tertiary deposits . . .
>   —Ten minutes before the invention of money . . .[19]

In this way, though with variations in style and tone, McGrath, like Rukeyser and LeSueur, provided perspective on and connections with nonviolent struggles of the Great Depression and those of the later period.

5

Conscientious Objection and Civil Rights
1940–1965

Martin Luther King's brand of radicalism can be traced to . . .
the lives and the teachings of Christ and Gandhi, the thinking
of Thoreau, the aborted hopes of James Farmer and A. Philip
Randolph, the tough strategy talks of Bayard Rustin.

—Vincent Harding[1]

One of the richest periods for the
nonviolent tradition in literature coincided, ironically, with wartime. It
began with writings by draft resisters during the first peacetime conscription in U.S. history, in 1940, and continued through the Second
World War, the Korean War, and the early years of the Vietnam War.
These writings told stories of conscientious objectors, nuclear pacifists,
and civil disobedients—several of whom were well-known poets and novelists either directly involved in or personally supportive of nonviolent
movements.

Writers who spent time in Civilian Public Service camps as C.O.s or
in prison as resisters during World War II included William Everson
(Brother Antoninus)(1912–1990), William Stafford (1914–1993), J. F.
Powers (b. 1917), and Robert Lowell (1917–1977), as well as activists
and scholars such as Mulford Sibley (1912–1989), David Dellinger
(b. 1915), and Gordon Zahn (b. 1918). Other well-known conscientious
objectors included James Farmer (b. 1920), who founded the Congress
of Racial Equality (CORE), a major force in resisting segregation, and
Kenneth Rexroth (1905–1982), who served as an important link between
poets and nonviolent activists of the 1930s and the San Francisco Renaissance of the 1950s and 1960s.

Although World War II is commonly regarded as a "popular" war, thousands in the United States refused to take up arms. Among the estimated fifty thousand "refusers" were twelve thousand conscientious objectors who spent time in Civilian Public Service camps; twenty-five thousand to fifty thousand who performed medical or other noncombatant service in the armed forces; and another six thousand or so who went to jail as outright resisters.[2] As during World War I, not all Americans regarded "killing the killers in order to stop the killing," in Brayton Shanley's memorable phrase, as the best and only choice.

Following the "radical" 1930s—significant in the contributions of the United Auto Workers and the Catholic Worker movement to nonviolence —major developments centered on resistance to the draft and to the nuclear arms race. Little by little, nonviolent activists took up Peter Maurin's challenge in his essay "Peace Preparedness," from the April 1938 *Catholic Worker:*

> They are increasing armaments
> in the fallacious hope that they
> will preserve peace by preparing for war.
> Before 1914 they prepared for war and got it.
> Nations have too long prepared
> for war, it is about time they prepared for peace.

Among various stories, the one involving resisters jailed in Danbury (Conn.) Federal Prison in 1940 became central to the lore of the peace movement in the decades that followed.

As with most draft refusers or resisters since the Civil War, the men at Danbury had refused military service on religious grounds. Unlike those who accepted the lawful alternative provided by the Selective Service System, they could not, in conscience, cooperate with the Selective Service System in any way. Jim Bristol, for example, viewed conscription "as hurtful to the United States; it was undemocratic and totalitarian. It denied the validity of moral and religious values."[3] Although Bristol, a Lutheran pastor, and David Dellinger, a divinity student at Union Theological Seminary, qualified for deferments, both went to jail as outright resisters. Even those who chose the conscientious objector's option came to regard Civilian Public Service as "involuntary servitude without compensation, nothing more than a program of slave labor offered by the State as an alternative to outright imprisonment."[4]

Once in Danbury prison, Dellinger, Jim Peck, and others found it necessary to resist policies of the criminal justice system, as Ammon Hennacy had done under similar circumstances at Atlanta Federal Prison during World War I. Leading a strike against racial segregation and other repressive practices, Danbury resisters landed in solitary confinement—"in the hole." Even there, their nonviolent protest continued in a hunger strike. Although the authorities offered the resisters several deals, including a personal bribe from the warden, they persisted. Eventually, they won the release not only of their coresisters, but also of all prisoners confined to the hole. The efforts of a man named Benedict, who refused pardon until it was extended to the group, constitute a legendary tale of resistance for justice's sake.

Howard Schoenfeld, Benedict's compatriot, described the resisters' release from solitary confinement, as they rejoined the other prisoners:

> We straggled across the empty yard, basking in the sun, enjoying our freedom. A spontaneous wave of applause broke out among the [regular prisoners] as the first of our group entered the [mess] hall. Surging across the hall, the waves became a crescendo. Six hundred pairs of hands joined in and the crescendo became pandemonium . . . but when the so-called criminals who had been in solitary came in, the convicts literally went wild, beating their metal cups on the tables, and stamping their feet. We stood in the center of the hall, astounded at the demonstration. It became clear that although they were applauding Benedict, Brooks and all of us who had been in solitary, they were doing something more. A mass catharsis of human misery was taking place before our eyes. Some of the men were weeping, other were laughing like madmen. It was like nothing I had ever seen before, and nothing I ever expect to see again.[5]

This story resembles many others involving those who found it impossible to bear arms during wartime, in the ongoing experience and education of nonviolent activists. Not surprisingly, much of the leadership of U.S. Quakerism after the war came from those who served in prison and in Civilian Public Service camps and units; several of them, including Dellinger and Peck, became essential activists, theorists, and strategists for civil rights and antiwar movements later on.

When the United States entered the war against Japan and Germany in 1941, thousands of conscientious objectors enlisted under a provision for alternate service written into the 1940 draft law. That provision, respecting the conscience of those with religious or philosophical objections to killing, had not been achieved easily. The effort of peace churches to win recognition from the government had preceded the founding of the new nation; during the First American Congress in 1789, James Madison proposed that "no person religiously scrupulous of bearing arms shall be compelled to render military service in person." In subsequent wars, some provisions were made for individual registrants, but no general policy existed until 1940; even then, it was randomly ignored and applied by local draft boards.

Although many young men came to conscientious objection as a result of religious upbringing or membership in pacifist organizations during the 1930s, others—Stanley Kunitz (b. 1905), Gordon Zahn, and Robert Lowell—arrived at their positions on their own. Zahn, who as a youngster entertained heroic fantasies of making a dramatic refusal to take part in war, pictured himself "as being the only Catholic to do so." This may have been because his public school education had made him more aware than a parochial school education would have done of Catholicism's "often enough *culpable* involvement with wars of past history."[6]

A well-known poet and editor and, because of his age, barely eligible for the draft, Kunitz agreed with his contemporaries that Hitler must be stopped, but Kunitz could not, in conscience, kill to accomplish that purpose. Like others who found themselves in this dilemma, Kunitz decided to seek a 1-A-0 classification (a conscientious objector in uniform). In "Reflection by a Mailbox," from *Passport to a War* (1944), he wrote of the agonizing period, as he waited

> under the hemlock by the road
> For the red-haired postman with the smiling hand
> To bring me my passport to the war.[7]

Once it had him in uniform, the military system "punished" the thirty-eight-year-old recruit by making him dig latrines for several years. Near the end of the war, when a literary magazine he edited won first prize in an "all army" competition, the army transferred Kunitz to a Washington, D.C., office and offered him a commission, which he turned down.

This extended encounter with the military—the state's emissary—influenced Kunitz's life and writing, and in several important poems of the postmodernist period, he explored the conflict between individual conscience and the politics of the status quo. In a poem and an essay written during the Vietnam War, "Around Pastor Bonhoeffer" and "Poet and State," Kunitz returned to issues that provoked his earlier war resistance.

The poem dramatizes the dilemma of a nonviolent activist in the face of evil. The conscience of Dietrich Bonhoeffer, a German Lutheran theologian, "forced him, against the pacific temper of his spirit . . . to join in a conspiracy for the murder of Hitler." The poem speaks of "midnight bells / jangling" in Pastor Bonhoeffer's ears:

if you permit
this evil, what is the good
of the good of your life?

When the plot against Hitler failed, Bonhoeffer, his brother, and their associates were jailed. The final section of the poem describes Bonhoeffer as he meets his fate:

> Round-faced, bespectacled, mild,
> candid with costly grace,
> he walked toward the gallows
> and did not falter.

By this mysterious act, Bonhoeffer, going against everything he believed, nonetheless entered a beloved community where God

> would take him by the shoulder, . . .
> and turn him round
> to face his brothers in the world.[8]

Kunitz, having responded to evil by rejecting violence, understood Bonhoeffer's agony in going against his own principles. Both men refused, in Gandhi's words, to use nonviolence as an excuse for cowardice.

In "Poet and State," initially a lecture at the Cooper Union, Kunitz explored a theme similar to the one in the poem, "the connection between good government and right words." Although a poet knows "that revolutions of sensibility are not won at the barricades," he knows also that *not* acting may be more disastrous, in the long run, than acting precipitously or unwisely. When the hour is late, Kunitz added, "some refusals are no longer permitted him, lest he wither at the heart."

In describing the traditional conflict between "poet" and "state," Kunitz focused on a dilemma central to the writings of literary radicals past and present. An artist stays "healthy in a sick world," he argues, by working to sustain that continuous though tenuous network uniting everything in nature—"touch it at any point, and the whole web shudders"; and by serving not those who make history, but those subject to it—"to whom can one pledge one's allegiance," he asks rhetorically, "except to the victims?"[9]

Assuming these responsibilities, as artist and person, Kunitz lives, as with others committed to nonviolence, in conflict with the established

order and with the risks involved with that attitude. "In a murderous
time," as he says in "The Testing Tree":

> the heart breaks and breaks
> and lives by breaking.
> It is necessary to go
> through dark and deeper dark
> and not to turn.[10]

Although not an activist in the conventional sense—he neither burned
draft files nor committed civil disobedience—Kunitz remains a persistent,
eloquent voice against the warmaking state. He has recalled with pride,
also, that poets who told the ghastly truth about Vietnam long before the
public had ears for it and who converted the White House Arts Festival
on July 14, 1965, into a public protest against Lyndon Johnson's war
policies helped to strengthen the antiwar movement.

That White House incident involved Kunitz's friend and compatriot,
Robert Lowell, who had become the most visible "literary personality" of
his generation, in part, because of his widely publicized draft resistance
during World War II. A *New York Times* headline in September 1943,
"To Act on Draft Evader," announced the initial indictment of the prom-
ising young poet, member of a famous New England family, and recent
convert to Roman Catholicism. Later, in "Memories of West Street and
Lepke," he described his experience as "a fire-breathing C.O., . . . telling
off the state and the president" and serving time in a New York City jail
and in Danbury Federal Prison.[11] When his cellmate, *Murder Incorpo-
rated*'s Czar Lepke, said to Lowell, "I'm in for killing. What are you in
for?," Lowell replied, "Oh, I'm in for refusing to kill." According to Jim
Peck, a well-known activist with the War Resisters' League, "Lepke burst
out laughing."[12]

Although he had volunteered previously for military service, Lowell
changed his mind by the time his induction notice arrived from the Selective Service. In a "Declaration of Personal Responsibility," sent directly
to President Franklin Roosevelt, Lowell said that he "must refuse the
opportunity you offer me . . . in the Armed Forces." Acknowledging that
the United States undertook "a patriotic war to preserve *our lives, our
fortunes, and our sacred honor* against the lawless aggressions of a totalitarian league," he accused the country, by 1943, of "collaborating with the
most unscrupulous and powerful dictatorships to destroy law, freedom,
democracy, and above all, our continued national sovereignty."

In taking this stand, Lowell challenged traditional justifications for making war, in language that anticipates official statements that would be adopted by the Roman Catholic hierarchy forty years later. He called attention, for example, to "rumors of the staggering civilian casualties that had resulted from the mining of the Ruhr Dams" and later reports of "the razing of Hamburg, where 200,000 non-combatants are reported dead, after an almost apocalyptic series of all-out air raids." In light of that change in the manner of conducting the war, Lowell said, "I have come to the conclusion that I cannot participate in a war whose prosecution, as far as I can judge, constitutes a betrayal of my country."[13]

Sentenced to a year and a day, though released earlier, Lowell later raised similar objections to the Vietnam War. He appears as a central figure in Mailer's *The Armies of the Night* (chap. 6) about the 1967 march on Washington, which became the subject of several poems describing his involvement. At one point, he

> sat in the sunset
> shade of our Bastille, the Pentagon,
> nursing leg- and arch-cramps, my cowardly,
> foolhardy heart;

as the military police "tiptoed through us / in single file, and then the second wave / trampled us flat and back."[14]

Saturation bombing, similar to that employed by the Allies at Hamburg and mentioned in Lowell's letter to Roosevelt, provoked angry, powerful indictments of modern warfare by later war resisters. A popular antiwar novel, Kurt Vonnegut's *Slaughterhouse Five; or, The Children's Crusade* (1970), for example, dramatizes the truth of Lowell's argument about the thousands of noncombatant deaths, this time in British and American air raids on Dresden. The year before, in an eloquent testimony regarding his own "conversion" to nonviolence, Philip Berrigan, a paratrooper during World War II before becoming a war resister, said that a V-E Day tour of another German city, Munster—an "urban desert . . . this sheer, incomprehensible ruin"—contributed to his destroying draft files and similar activities after 1965.[15] For Berrigan, the direct relationship between the use of sophisticated weapons of mass destruction and an increase in civilian deaths underscored the horror of modern war. In World War I, 95 percent of those killed in war were soldiers, 5 percent were civilians; in World War II, 52 percent were soldiers, 48 percent were civilians; in the Korean War, 16 percent were soldiers, 84 percent were civilians.

The most powerful statement in verse supporting draft resistance during World War II was written by someone on active duty, Lowell's friend and contemporary, Karl Shapiro (b. 1913). Composed while he was a soldier in the South Pacific, "The Conscientious Objector" appeared in *V-Letter and Other Poems* (1944), much of it based upon Shapiro's army experience. A "definition" poem, resembling other Shapiro poems of this period—notably "Auto Wreck," "Drug Store," and "University"—"The Conscientious Objector" is a moving tribute to the persistent, faithful peace witness of conscientious objectors in prison.

In a cluster of metaphors and statements, the poem conveys something of the history of conscientious objection and of a three-centuries-old counterculture associated with the nonviolent tradition in the United States. Building on the image of the prison as a ship, "the decks, the catwalks, and the narrow light," the poem calls the C.O.s a "mutinous crew," rather like the revolutionary Puritans and similar missionaries passionate about a "new" theology,

> Troubling the captains for plain decencies,
> A Mayflower brim with pilgrims headed out
> To establish new theocracies to west . . .
> Like all men hunted from the world you made
> A good community, voyaging the storm
> To no safe Plymouth or green Ararat;

Although subject to criticism from those fighting a "popular" war, C.O.s had obviously won the respect of the spokesperson, someone actively engaged in combat:

> Well might the soldier kissing the hot beach
> Erupting in his face damn all your kind.
> Yet you who saved neither yourselves nor us
> Are equally with those who shed the blood
> The heroes of our cause. Your conscience is
> What we come back to in the armistice.[16]

The final statement, a powerful and unexpected tribute to conscience, is prophetic, in light of the moral leadership that James Farmer, Dellinger, Peck, and other C.O.s provided in the postwar years.

Two extraordinary memoirs focusing on conscientious objection during World War II were by another award-winning poet, William Stafford, and a sociologist, Gordon Zahn, whose writings would redirect American

Catholic thought about war and peace in the next generation among the hierarchy and some laity.

Down in My Heart (1947) is Stafford's brief, understated, yet moving story of his experience among those who could (or would) not take up arms, even against Hitler. Focusing on his years in Civilian Public Service camps "managed" by the peace churches, Stafford's book dramatizes the confusion and loneliness of the objectors, as well as the sense of community that they came to value for themselves and others. "Down in our hearts we found it," he wrote in retrospect, "and wanted to protect and promote it as something more important than—something prerequisite to—any geographical kinship or national loyalty." [17]

In one episode at an Arkansas camp, a potentially violent confrontation emerged between war resisters and a hostile band of locals, during the C.O.s infrequent visit to a nearby town. Grabbing a copy of Whitman's *Leaves of Grass,* being read by a C.O., a member of the civilian posse expressed skepticism about anyone reading such unrhymed "poetry," as others threatened the men and searched them for possible security information. Fortunately, a local deputy arrived to dissipate the crowd before any violence broke out. In such incidents, including racial and class conflicts that erupted in the camp, the C.O.s learned about resolving the conflicts that characterize life on or off the battlefield. In the process, they decided where they must draw the line in relationship to the warmaking state—cooperating here, resisting there—and how they might sustain themselves, while living in conflict with the dominant culture.

The principal "voice" in *Down in My Heart* chooses a kind of *via media* between citizen involvement and total resistance. The book, in fact, is a kind of extended justification, an *apologia pro vita sua,* addressed to "George," a fellow C.O. who found that he could not, in conscience, go along with the government-approved program for alternative service. In prison, he winds up in the hole on a hunger strike (like the activists, later, in Mailer's *Armies of the Night*), "protesting the continued imprisonment of men who would not kill and the continued drafting of men for the purpose of killing."

George's "total resistance" both repels and fascinates the narrator; it was, he says, a life "no longer tied to considerations of policy, personal prestige, or the endless decisions, diplomacies, and hopes of ordinary social living," though with "the exhilarations of the outlaw, his personal freedoms, and his constant living with rebellion." [18] The narrator chooses a more conventional route—as did Stafford, following the war—for reasons implied in his conversation with George.

For aesthetic and historical reasons, this "insider's" view of a peace community in wartime occupies a central place in this literary tradition. A chapter called "We Built a Bridge" suggests, among other things, an important new direction for nonviolence in the United States during the 1940s, as it began to build on traditions from other religions and cultures, and to pay closer attention to "inner experience." In one episode, a C.O. named Ken spent a week-long furlough among a group of pacifists at Trabuco College, "a new group of unpopulated buildings, isolated, unadvertised, in the hills of southern California." There, he read and discussed Taoism and St. Augustine, in the company of two influential teachers and writers from England, Aldous Huxley and Gerald Heard, and a Christian mystic, Allan Hunter. They practiced "a pattern of living designed to promote mental, or mystical experience," with Heard stressing the importance of accepting responsibility "for what goes on between ourselves and others."[19]

These exiles and the community around them had immersed themselves in Buddhist and Hindu religious disciplines and literature and the nonviolent tradition associated with them. Huxley, Heard, and later Christopher Isherwood, pacifist and elder statesman to the gay liberation movement, constituted a kind of think tank for nonviolence during the war years, much as Lady Ottoline Morrell's Garsington Manor did for pacifists and resisters during the First World War. And although their writings belong to the literary history of their native country, they made important contributions to the nonviolent tradition in American literature as well. Gore Vidal, who has skillfully traced the decline of the American empire since 1950, regarded Isherwood as "the greatest prose writer in English." Similarly, the influence of Huxley and Heard is evident in the literary and political writings of Allen Ginsberg, Gary Snyder, and others associated with the San Francisco Renaissance, but Stafford's memoir provides the best rendering of the subtlety and the power of this "English" contribution to the American tradition of nonviolence in this period.

The importance of Gordon Zahn's memoir, *Another Part of the War* (1979), grows, similarly, out of his significant professional and personal influence on a relatively new element of the tradition. His background is not one of the traditional peace churches, but the Roman Catholic Church, which, except for the Catholic Worker movement, contributed little to nonviolent theory and practice before this period. Although individual members and particular texts associated with Catholicism had been important since 1933—from Peter Maurin's "Easy Essays" and Dorothy Day's memoirs—the writings of Gordon Zahn extended the "nonviolence gospel" to a larger community of Catholics. To this literary line also belong the essays and poems by the clergymen Thomas Merton and Daniel Berrigan, as well as various writings by William Everson, Michael Harrington, James Forest, James Douglass, and a host of statements by younger activists indebted to them.

Zahn's memoir, more sociological than literary, tells the story of Camp Simon, near Weaver and Stoddard, New Hampshire, during World War II, "the first corporate witness against war and military service in the history of American Catholicism."[20] Interspersed with personal reflections and occasional work songs that parody traditional militarist hymns, the story is told with a novelist's eye, reminiscent of *The Enormous Room* by e. e. cummings. At Camp Simon, anarchists and pacifists shared quarters with the reactionary and sometime anti-Semitic followers of Father Charles E. Coughlin, a Detroit priest active during the depression. Recognizing personal foibles of the participants, the narrator appreciates their courage nonetheless, at a time when the prevailing militarist mentality posed an almost universal threat to the mind and sensibility of many. Although there were "no brutal games, no barbed wire, no dongs, no gas chambers" at Camp Simon, it resembled primitive and repressive jails "inspired by and conducted under de facto military authority." An agency of the Selective Service System, with the church's help it kept objectors invisible, as Zahn says, and suppressed a religious minority in time of war.[21]

Before the publication of his memoir, Zahn had already established important links between war resistance and Catholic social teachings. In 1952, he "shook up" the ecclesiastical establishment by writing a careful study that documented Catholic complicity in Hitler's rise to power. The unspoken warning in *German Catholics and Hitler's War* was that American Catholics tolerating nuclear weapons and a warmaking state behaved as "good Germans," in a way that clearly violated the basic teaching of the just-war theory and more recent social encyclicals.

Zahn's next book, a biography of Franz Jaggerstatter, a German war resister, addressed not only the individual Catholic's right to conscientious objection, according to Thomas Merton, but also "the question of the Church's own mission of protest and prophecy" in the gravest spiritual crisis in human history.[22] Later activists and writers who acknowledged an indebtedness to Zahn's writings include Philip Berrigan, in his memoir, *Punishment for Peace* (1969); Robert Bly, in an essay entitled "Leaping Into Political Poetry" (1970); and Daniel Berrigan, in his play, *The Trial of the Catonsville Nine* (1970). James Harney, a priest from Boston, tells in his preface to a later edition of the Jaggerstatter biography that Zahn's book influenced Harney's own decision to burn draft records in Milwaukee, as it did other members of the "ultra-resistance" who participated in

Plowshares actions after 1980. Many nonviolent activists justified their "disarming" nuclear missiles on grounds of international law, including judgments handed down against Nazi war criminals at the Nuremberg trials and similar judgments implicit in Zahn's criticism of the church hierarchy in Nazi Germany.

More popular than Zahn's writings, though no more profound in their influence, are the later poems and essays of Thomas Merton (1915–1968). Author of a popular book about his becoming a Trappist, *The Seven Storey Mountain* (1948), and numerous religious tracts, Merton turned his considerable literary skills, in the early 1960s, to articles and pamphlets advocating support for civil rights and antinuclear movements. They began with "The Root of War Is Fear," *Catholic Worker* (October 1961), and included the introduction to an important anthology, *Breakthrough to Peace: Twelve Views on the Threat of Thermonuclear Extermination* (1962), which appeared not long after the superior general of the Cistercian Order forbad him to write on war and peace.

Merton's many poems and essays on this theme, including the posthumously published collection, *The Nonviolent Alternative* (1974), have had considerable effect on his large reading public. In a long introduction to the latter volume, Gordon Zahn argued that "Merton had set out to correct what he recognized to be a short-sighted and essentially unchristian attitude that threatened to bring about a total disaster for Church, nation, and world." In doing so, his voice was surprisingly influential, and "decisive enough at least to have him silenced."[23]

Merton's most important essays, "Blessed Are the Meek: The Christian Roots of Nonviolence" and "War and the Crisis of Language"—similar in theme to Orwell's "Politics and the English Language"—are a kind of "anguished lament," as Zahn argued, "over the almost total lack of protest on the part of religious people and clergy, in the face of enormous social evils." Although Merton never risked jail by committing civil disobedience or dismantling nuclear weapons, he provoked others to take such radical action. Among those participating in a religious retreat that he conducted at the Trappist monastery in Kentucky in November 1964, for example, were Daniel Berrigan, Philip Berrigan, James Forest, Tom Cornell, and Robert Cunnane—all of whom ended up in prison within the next four years, for burning draft files.

In addition to an impressive body of writings by people already mentioned, a number of individual works after 1945, "the year of the bomb," dramatize American literature's preoccupation—one might say obsession—with the fragile nature of public and private life in these United States. Long before sociological studies documented the collapse of "community" in national life, artists and critics talked about the shadow side of American culture as it manifested itself following World War II. Some of their preoccupations were traditional ones, which have informed or haunted American artists since the first European settlements—a new Adam in an unknown wilderness and relationships between white people and people of color. Other preoccupations were new to artists of the imperial nation (or to use a designation commonly associated with the period, "to postmodernism"), particularly the political and psychological effects of the nuclear bomb.

Reed Whittemore's sardonic, yet witty "Reflections upon a Recurrent Suggestion by Civil Defense Authorities That I Build a Bombshelter in My Backyard" is an early work indicating the psychological effect of the threat posed by nuclear weapons on the public consciousness—or at least one consciousness. Written in the mid-1950s, as government agencies advocated citizens' defending themselves by "digging" their own private shelters, the poem was rejected by *The New Yorker* as "no longer timely" at that point, but was later published elsewhere and widely reprinted. After thinking seriously about this nutty proposal, the speaker eventually dismisses it, sensibly equating the construction of such shelters with playing games.

As a child, one might pretend that one was safe "from the world's hurt" in a backyard dugout. Facing the bomb, however, the speaker refuses to play, this time, according to "new and terrible rules of romance":

> But I'll not, no, not do it, not go back
> And lie there in that dark under the weight
> Of all that earth on that old door for my state.
> I know too much to think now that, if I creep
> From the grown-up's house to the child's house,
>   I'll keep.

The narrator's "refusing to go along with what comes along" resembles the behavior of a man in southern Illinois during the Cuban missile crisis, when President John F. Kennedy and Premier Nikita Khrushchev took the United States and the Soviet Union to the brink of war. An "ordinary citizen," he simply walked through the city square with a large handmade sign saying, "NO!" Such acts of resistance, recounted in numerous poems of the period, were minimalist assertions of humanity in an inhuman environment, long before large-scale demonstrations against nuclear armaments, numbering between four hundred thousand and one million people, were common throughout the world. Commenting once on

"Reflections," Reed Whittemore said that he might not follow his own instructions "in an emergency, but I like to think I would; so the poem gives me a pleasant image of me as I would like to be."[24]

Finding words to communicate the immediacy of the nuclear threat in prose or poetry was no simple task, particularly as literary and academic establishments ignored or denied their complicity in the making, manufacturing, and deployment of weapons or simply pretended that the threat was not there. No wonder that—as the literary critic, Terrence Des Pres, argued—cynicism, despair, and "an allegiance to a mystique of physical force" dominated much public discourse, in both popular and "high" culture.[25] In individual works resembling Whittemore's, several writers found an appropriate voice for anguish in "an age of anxiety." Gradually, haltingly, they then moved toward affirming another set of values in concrete, vivid statements, while living "in a dark time."

In perhaps the most ambitious, and certainly the most influential, poem of the postwar period, Allen Ginsberg faced the personal alienation and discontinuity associated with a postwar, nuclear age. The opening line of his long poem *Howl* (1955) describes the general complaint: "I saw the best minds of my generation destroyed by madness." The consequences of this destruction are the subject of the three main sections of the poem, with the principal cause of that condition named in "Footnote": "Moloch whose fate is a cloud of sexless hydrogen." In total effect, *Howl* moves beyond an indictment of war and violence to some suggestion of how to survive in a world on the edge of the abyss, perhaps even how to redeem it or at least to redirect one's own life.

Taking the reaction to *Howl* as a measure of its importance in literary and political history, one can hardly overestimate the poem's success. It helped to initiate a long-overdue conversation on the implications of the nuclear age—moral, social, aesthetic; and because of Ginsberg's commitment to and association with nonviolent social change, the poem led to the recovery of earlier writings and literary links associated with the nonviolent tradition. Ginsberg's poem evoked renewed interest in Walt Whitman, for example, after a general neglect of him by the generation of Eliot and Pound. In his testimony on behalf of the Chicago Eight, Ginsberg reminded people of Whitman's central place in espousing democratic values, including his argument that "the attitude of great poets is to cheer up slaves and horrify despots."

In fiction, Bernard Malamud, Gore Vidal, James Baldwin, Norman Mailer, Joseph Heller, and others also fashioned a prose idiom and images exposing an imperial age's form and pressure. Although early postmodernist poems and novels—Randall Jarrell's "Death of the Ball Turret Gunner" and Mailer's *Naked and the Dead*—describe the cruelty and chaos of war somewhat in the antiwar mode of the early modernist writings about World War I, Ginsberg's *Howl* and Heller's *Catch-22* (1961) expose the structural violence of a military culture and the destabilization of a nation dominated by a military-industrial-university complex. They portray the sardonic, multidimensional atmosphere of an aggressive, dominating culture; and their indictments of the lasting effect of war and of warmaking focus on the deeper, more pervasive implications of an ethics of violence. As *Catch-22* and several Vietnam novels indicate, war casualties continue to pile up long after the last shot is fired because of the physical and psychological wounds endured. The number of U.S. veterans of the Vietnam War to die by suicide exceeds the number of casualties by combat.

As these antiwar writings appeared, another important movement associated with nonviolence was in the making. Although generally thought of as beginning with the Montgomery bus boycott, the civil rights movement actually began some years before the fateful day of December 1, 1955 in Montgomery, Alabama, when one African American woman was "just too tired" to obey a state law requiring her to give up her seat to a white man. Rosa Parks's resistance was an act of personal courage, but it had been prepared for by a campaign of education and action that began in the 1940s.

James Farmer, former C.O. and race-relations secretary of the Fellowship of Reconciliation (FOR), had referred to the campaign as "The Brotherhood Mobilization," in recommending a well-organized campaign against segregation in the North in 1942. In memoranda to A. J. Muste, executive director of FOR, Farmer spelled out the conditions and time plan for "a distinctive and radical approach" by pacifists and nonpacifists. The following year, a group in Chicago adapted the sit-in strategy used by labor organizers during the depression, and formed a national organization, the Congress of Racial Equality (CORE). Its "Rules for Action" included guarantees that a CORE member "will investigate the facts carefully before determining whether or not racial injustice exists in a given situation; will make a sincere effort to avoid malice and hatred toward any group or individual; and will never use malicious slogans or labels to discredit any opponent."[26]

From these early plans came various forms of direct action, including the freedom rides, a phenomenon of the early 1960s, but actually initiated as "the Journey of Reconciliation" in April 1947, "to devise techniques for eliminating Jim Crow in travel, but also as a training ground for similar peaceful projects against discrimination in such major areas as employment and in the armed services."[27] Eight African Americans and eight white men—including Bayard Rustin, Conrad Lynn, George Houser, Jim Peck, and members of FOR, American Friends Service Committee (AFSC), and the War Resisters League (WRL)—rode Greyhound and Trailways buses throughout the South to test a recent Supreme Court decision outlawing segregation in interstate travel. Several of these "freedom riders" were arrested, jailed, and beaten; and Rustin served twenty-three days on a chain gang in North Carolina.

Records and brief transcripts of this early organizing, by these and other members of FOR, AFSC, and WRL, are among the most valuable writings on applying Gandhian principles to various campaigns. Rustin, Houser, and Glenn Smiley, also with FOR, who lent their experience and knowledge to Martin Luther King, Jr., soon after he began his first campaign in Montgomery, Alabama, stand with him as some of the great teachers in the history of nonviolence.

Because the civil rights movement's push for social change coincided with the emergence of the United States as the world's major economic and military power, a number of important "power" issues emerged in the literature of this period. In this discussion, the writings of two African Americans—one a major literary figure of the period, James Baldwin, and the other, Malcolm X (1925–1965), a dramatic counterpoint to Martin Luther King—must be mentioned, even if both expressed reservations about nonviolence.

To be born black in "a white country, an Anglo-Teutonic, antisexual country," as James Baldwin described the United States, meant something. And although Baldwin maintained some distance from the movement (as a Northerner, he said, he knew little about the South), he wrote incisively about the various misuses of power that left African Americans and others disenfranchised a century after the Emancipation Proclamation. In *The Fire Next Time* (1961), for example, he described white people who "had robbed black people of their liberty and who profited by this theft every hour that they lived."

> They had the judges, the juries, the shotguns, the law—in a word, power. But it was a criminal power, to be feared but not respected, and to be outwitted in any way whatever.[28]

At such times, Baldwin's rhetoric closely resembled that of Malcolm X, whose remarkable life and leadership became associated with the "black power" movement, as a primary strategy for social change. At other times, Baldwin's program for "what must be done" to stop white people from beating African Americans over the head "every instant of our brief passage on the planet" closely resembled Martin Luther King's.

Cautioning African Americans against the self-destructive legacies of racial hatred, Baldwin argued, for example, that white American he-men were totally unprepared "for anything that could not be settled with a club or a fist or a gun." The struggle to resolve racial conflict, "involving the historical role of Christianity in the realm of power—that is, politics —and in the realm of morals," he said, will end successfully only when white people learn "to accept and love themselves and each other—which will not be tomorrow and may very well be never."[29]

Although Malcolm X and Martin Luther King Jr. are regarded as complementary and essential to social change in this period, the task of addressing these psychological and political issues through nonviolence is rightly associated with the life and writings of King. Now recognized nationally and internationally as the principal figure in nonviolence in this period, if not in U.S. history, King, with the help of many talented and skilled associates in the civil rights movement, reclaimed an American tradition by bringing back to this country an approach to resisting injustice and to reconciling conflict that Woolman, Garrison, and Ballou had initiated earlier.

Shortly after he became involved in the Montgomery bus boycott in 1955, King emphasized the importance of a total nonviolent campaign, in the Garrisonian and Gandhian manner. Among several essential essays, his "Letter from Birmingham Jail" (1963) reflects the basic rationale for the civil rights movement and the nonviolent approach informing it. For that reason, among others, it remains one of the most important documents in this literary history, reprinted thousands of times in many languages and now a standard selection in essay anthologies. Its reference point is religious, particularly Christian, the rhetoric of which King shared with his audience. In the process of writing the essay, however, King purged and purified the conventional language of religion, making his argument accessible even to those who did not share his background.

Specifically, "Letter from Birmingham Jail" challenged those who counseled "nonviolence" yet did nothing to alleviate the suffering of those enduring injustice. The argument is supported with a vivid account from King's own life that catalogs the indignities and anxieties associated with being a black person, a parent, a son, or a daughter who endured injustice simply because of the color of his or her skin. Addressed to Southern clergyman who had criticized King for "causing trouble" in the most segregated city in America, the "Letter" is also a brilliant, brief summary of how to conduct a nonviolent campaign, the steps necessary to preparing for it, and its ultimate goal: reconciliation among all people.

A skilled preacher, King employs in his "Letter," as in most of his writings, language that is simple and direct, yet very sophisticated in its use of theological and philosophical discourse. He refers to and draws upon a whole history of religious thought, from Augustine and Aquinas to Reinhold Niebuhr and Paul Tillich. It is also a powerful answer to and refutation of Niebuhr's criticism of pacifism, a cause célèbre of the 1930s. A student and admirer of Niebuhr's writings on social ethics, King outlines in this essay, and later in "Declaration of Independence from the War in Vietnam," why someone must stop the killing, no matter what the circumstance, no matter what the cost.

Although other writings of the period, including King's "Loving Your Enemies," elaborate on and deepen the basic teachings of nonviolence, "Letter from Birmingham Jail" reflects "new beginnings" for nonviolence, with enormous implications for the immediate future, particularly for Cesar Chavez and Dolores Huerta's effort on behalf of itinerant farm workers and the movement against the war in Vietnam, as well as the women's movement and resistance to the nuclear arms race.

In the late 1950s, while Baldwin, King, and LeRoi Jones (Amiri Baraka) were among those poets, novelists, and essayists who focused on issues related to civil rights, other writers made connections between that movement and their concerns about the nuclear arms race and imperial policies of the American government. Among those significant for the nonviolent tradition were poets Paul Goodman, Muriel Rukeyser, Thomas McGrath, Denise Levertov, Allen Ginsberg, and Robert Bly; pamphleteers David Dellinger, Martin Luther King Jr., and Barbara Deming; scholars Mulford Sibley, Vincent Harding, Staughton Lynd; and songwriters Pete Seeger, Phil Ochs, Joan Baez, and Utah Phillips. Their work reflects the strength of the tradition, which includes many small, communal actions against nuclear testing, the draft, and the war, in the early years of Vietnam.

The San Francisco-to-Moscow peace walk of 1961 and the later continental walk of 1976, described in Charlie King's song "Do the Continental Walk" ("Stop building H-bombs / And build a better home instead"), stressed the importance of a community's affirming a belief through personal and public testimony. In October 1961, after ten months of walking, thirty-one members of the Committee for Nonviolent Action, including Brad Lyttle, entered Red Square in Moscow after demonstrating for peace at military bases across the United States and Western Europe. (Beecher's poem "Engagement at the Salt Fork," quoted in the introduction, is a literary artifact from that pilgrimage.)

As a direct result of this effort, a series of demonstrations and public pronouncements followed, including the Quebec-to-Guantanamo walk of 1963–1964. The history of this action and the confrontation with Laurie

Pritchett, police chief of Albany, Georgia, is described in Barbara Deming's moving memoir, *Prison Notes* (1966), and alluded to in Pete Seeger's verse, adapted from an old protest song:

> No more Pritchett, no more Pritchett,
> No more Pritchett over me.
> And before I'll be a slave,
> I'll be buried in my grave,
> And go home to my Lord and be free.

As with the civil disobedience of Albert Bigelow, who sailed a thirty-foot boat, the *Golden Rule,* into the forbidden nuclear-testing area in the western Pacific in 1958, and Catholic Worker protests that ended the atomic-bomb drills in New York City about the same time, the 1961 Peace Walk brought the problem of atmospheric testing of atomic weapons to public attention. And as a result of a public outcry, that testing was eventually banned by the United States and the Soviet Union. Although public witness of this kind appears modest in the face of major social injustice or danger, during the last years of the cold war many Americans regarded a peace walk as "radical"; at the very least, these activities kept an antiwar tradition alive that militant "Cold Warriors" had forgotten about, had never heard of, or willfully denied.

At the same time, extended communities associated with earlier labor organizers, socialists, and pacifists in the Bay Area of California and in the Lower East Side of New York City initiated literary projects that made significant contributions to nonviolence just before and during the early years of the Vietnam War. The Beats (Allen Ginsberg, Lawrence Ferlinghetti, William Everson) around the City Lights Bookshop in San Francisco, the Fugs (Ed Sanders and Tuli Kupferberg) around the Peace Eye Bookstore in New York City, and Poets Against the War in Vietnam (Robert Bly and David Ray) from the Midwest kept alive a tradition associated with 1930s radicals like Muriel Rukeyser, Kenneth Rexroth, Meridel LeSueur, and Thomas McGrath.

Everson and Sanders had been associated with a persistent community of nonviolent activists around the War Resisters League and the Catholic Worker community in the California Bay Area and in the Lower East Side in New York City, respectively. Together, they provided an intellectual and artistic base for movement periodicals such as *Win, Liberation,* and *Evergreen Review,* as Bly and others did through *The Sixties* and other "little magazines" and impromptu "organizations."

The Fugs, a hilarious "folk ensemble of poets," and the Peace Eye

Bookstore, "cultural center and scrounge lounge popular in its day," were the creations of Sanders and his East Village associate, Tuli Kupferberg. Sanders became well-known as the publisher—"between police raids," as Martin Jezer has said—of *Fuck You: A Magazine of the Arts,* "dedicated to pacifism, unilateral disarmament, national defense through nonviolent resistance, multilateral indiscriminate apertural conjugation, anarchism, world federalism, civil disobedience, obstructors and submarine boarders, and all those groped by J. Edgar Hoover in the silent halls of Congress."[30]

At the time, many Americans, especially militant anticommunists, regarded Hoover as practically a saint; famous for "bashing" gays and lesbians, he was himself a homosexual, though only the Mafia, apparently, knew for sure. Sanders and Kupferberg's humor obviously contributed to their appeal and popularity among young dissidents, especially anyone facing the draft and the Vietnam War, and they drew many into the peace movement. Their antiwar masterpieces included satirical songs, "The Great Slum Goddess from the Lower East Side" and "Kill for Peace," and an outrageous pamphlet, *1001 Ways to the Beat the Draft* (1966), advising draft resisters to "4. Die." or "11. Start to menstruate. (Better red than dead)." or "108. Tell the security officer that you are a brother of Allen Ginsberg."[31]

Along the way, an alliance emerged that led eventually to another liberation movement. Since the late eighteenth century, radical politics and "pornography" (an inadequate term describing sexually explicit language and scenes formerly regarded as unprintable) had been allies. During the Revolution, for example, Americans favoring the colonists in the struggle against Great Britain paid for pirated editions of *Fanny Hill* that were published by political pamphleteers. In the late nineteenth century, Ezra Heywood and Angela Tilton, ardent abolitionists, nonresisters, and labor agitators (see chap. 3), went to jail for advocating "free love" ("Do you prefer paid love?" anarchists asked) and using sexually explicit language. Similarly, in the early 1960s, some nonviolent activists scandalized the public by publishing poems and graphics attacking the political and cultural status quo, from conscription to repression of gays, lesbians, and nudity. Following the Free Speech Movement in California, much of the activity centered in the East Village, New York City, where Allen Ginsberg lived and where Abby Hoffman first experimented successfully with street theater, in challenging the rhetoric of the Vietnam War. "Stonewall," an incident in which gays and lesbians actively resisted police oppression and harassment, took place in the same neighborhood a few years later.

Ed Sanders (b. 1939), poet and nonviolent activist, who walked a

650-mile stretch during the 1961 San Francisco-to-Moscow peace walk with the Committee for Nonviolent Action, has described this alliance and its socio-political-literary background. In addition to the freedom rides of 1961 and the assassination of John Kennedy and the Birmingham bombing of 1963, there were "the censors and those who would have banned eros from the American Imperium, the menace of J. Edgar Hoover and the Secret Police intermixed with decent police forces . . . who refused to allow America to become a right wing fortress, . . . the Mimeograph Revolution for poetry, the world of the underground film makers, and the rise of the Vietnam War in '64 and '65 as a national nightmare." In the middle of things, some people became aware of "oodles of freedom guaranteed by the United States Constitution that was not being used, . . . strengthened by the complex and beautiful trends of Beat/Objectivist Black Mountain poetry, modern painting, left wing politics and jazz."[32] In the East Village of the early 1960s, in other words, artists and political activists formed an alliance much like the one that had characterized Greenwich Village at the time of early modernism (1910–17).

The "education" of Ed Sanders resembles, moreover, the "education" of "exiles" from the Midwest who went to New York half a century earlier. Educated as a classicist, Sanders left his Kansas hometown in 1957 as "a direct result," he said, of reading Ginsberg's *Howl* in shop class and purchasing Ezra Pound's *Cantos*. The association between "nonviolence" and sexual explicitness, which characterized the lyrics of his musical group and of movement publications—as well as the hilarious street theater of Abbie Hoffman, hippies, and yippies—is evident in a poem of this period:

> The Cemetery Plot of Ed Sanders
> Shall Consist of:
>
> (a) a trophy case for Grail chasers
> (b) the jack off slab
> (c) the temple of the sneak fuck
> (d) the inscription chamber: Thank you mom & dad
> (e) the fane of nonviolence[33]

Not so coincidentally, one of the first largescale movements to challenge orthodox cold war "anticommunism" centered on language. The censorship trials over Ginsberg's *Howl*, that is, preceded protests against the House Un-American Activities Committee in San Francisco in 1960 and the Free Speech Movement in Berkeley, September 10, 1964, through January 4, 1965. During those years, Abbie Hoffman also made his first contribution to street theater at a meeting of patriots and veterans in his hometown, Worcester, Massachusetts, by unfurling a very large banner that read "FUCK COMMUNISM!"

The person most responsible for drawing the university community, faculty and students, into the movement against the war in the early 1960s, however, was Paul Goodman. As an editor of *Liberation* and author of numerous pamphlets, popular essays, and books—as teacher, visitor, and perpetual faculty-adviser to the student movement, he made a major contribution to vigorous public debate on the nature of American society. He came to national prominence with the publication of *Growing Up Absurd: Problems of Youth in an Alienated Society* (1960), which sold, at one point, over one hundred thousand copies a week, and he remained at the center of that discussion until his death twelve years later.

For this reason, and many others, Goodman—poet, novelist, psychologist, social and literary critic—occupies a special place in the nonviolent tradition in American literature. Rather like Paine and Garrison, Goodman popularized the ideas of principled dissent, of anarchism and communitarianism. As a man of letters, like Whitman, Goodman gave the counterculture of nonviolence a rich body of poems, stories, and essays informed by the spirit of the times. As a social philosopher—a kind of urban Thoreau, with *Communitas* (1947) his *Walden,* and the Hudson River his Walden Pond—Goodman preached a morality quite similar to that of the Concord transcendentalist: "Simplify, simplify, simplify." A characteristic sentence, beautiful in strength, perception, and good old American bawdy, summarizes the basic, modest goals for individual and society: "things like clean air and water, green grass, children with bright eyes, not being pushed around, useful work that suits one's abilities, plain tasty food, and occasional satisfactory nookie."[34] In his writing and on the platform, he issued a perpetual rallying cry that expressed the hopes and fears (eventually suppressed) of many American citizens.

In a torrent of essays, poems, stories, and articles for prestigious journals and movement newsletters, Goodman succeeded in naming what people sensed had been lost in the rush to empire and in the growth of the national security state. Identifying himself as a traditionalist, a child of the Reformation (Luther and Milton) and the Enlightenment (Kant, Paine, and Jefferson), he recommended what he called "dumb bunny" solutions to everyday problems, principally reclaiming their voices and taking initiative through nonviolent actions. Inevitably, he began with a direct challenge to individuals, whether ordinary citizens or corporate executives. In the preface to a collection of fugitive essays and letters to the editor, for example, he lamented the fact that so few Americans regarded themselves "as citizens, as society makers."

Instead they regard society as a pre-established machinery of institutions and authorities and they take themselves as I don't know what, some kind of individuals "in" society, whatever that means. Such a view is dangerous because it must result in a *few* people being society makers and exercising power over the rest. . . . The result must be and has been stupid standardization, stupid neglect, stupid injustice, and a base common denominator of valuation. There is no remedy except large numbers of authentic citizens, alert, concerned, intervening, deciding on all issues and all levels.[35]

Five years later, in 1967, before four hundred members of the National Security Industrial Association, Goodman issued this direct challenge to the NSIA membership, with an implied "manifesto" for nonviolent activists and a prophecy of the consequences of cold war policies:

You are the military-industrial [complex] of the United States, the most dangerous body of men at the present in the world, for you not only implement our disastrous policies but are an overwhelming lobby for them, and you expand and rigidify the wrong use of brains, resources, and labor so that change becomes difficult. Most likely the trends you represent will be interrupted by a shambles of riots, alienation, ecological catastrophes, wars, and revolutions, so that current long-range planning, including this conference, is irrelevant. But if we ask what *are* the technological needs and what ought to be researched in this coming period, . . . the best service that you people could perform is rather rapidly to phase yourselves out, passing on your relevant knowledge to people better qualified, or reorganizing yourselves with entirely different sponsors and commitments, so that you learn to think and feel in a different way. Since you are most of the [research and development] that there is, we cannot do without you as people, but we cannot do with you as you are.[36]

In essays and poems of this kind, Goodman made the nonviolent tradition visible and concrete for a large post-World War II audience, much as Paine, Garrison, Debs, and others had done for previous generations. That audience included a large and somewhat "new" contingency of college-educated men and women looking for a language to "name" what had been withheld from them, not "Nixon's elegant 'a piece of the action' but justice," as Gore Vidal said later. "Social justice."

Goodman's writings and speeches united thought and feeling in a way that drew people into the movement and sustained some of them through the dark and irresponsible period that followed the Vietnam War. Not surprisingly, in the middle of the Reagan/Bush years, some of Goodman's worst predictions about the collapse of the economy and the "infrastructure" came to pass.

Back of the antiwar movement, as Goodman understood, was that earlier manifestation of resistance to violence and injustice, the civil rights movement. What sometimes deteriorated into street theater or "media hype" by the mid-1970s had a solid base in the experience of organizers involved in voter registration campaigns in the South ten years earlier. At that time, Smiley, Farmer, Muste, Rustin, and King had inspired and trained thousands of people in social philosophy and strategy for social change. Individually and collectively, through the American Friends Service Committee and the Fellowship of Reconciliation, and the "new" Southern Christian Leadership Conference, these activists became central to the "counterculture" associated with an increasing number of efforts for justice and peace in the later third of the twentieth century.

6

War Resistance, Nuclear Disarmament, and Anti-imperialism
1965–1990

> Jefferson, Tom Paine, Garrison, Thoreau, A. J. Muste, the Freedom Riders, these are my countrymen whom I love; with them I take my stand.
>
> —Martin Jezer, 1967[1]

By 1967, poems, novels, and essays challenging U.S. cold war policies and priorities included work by writers committed to nonviolence (Muriel Rukeyser, Denise Levertov, and Allen Ginsberg), as well as by others of "the literary establishment" merely opposed to the Vietnam War (Mary McCarthy, Robert Lowell, and Norman Mailer). Even Edmund Wilson, that quintessential Parnassian and man of letters, whose contemporaries had long ago regretted their Wobblie or radical sympathies, took on the military-industrial complex by refusing to pay his income tax, as a protest against the arms race. In their multidimensional critique of war and violence, these writers extended the audience for, while documenting the effects of, nonviolent movements for social change.

At times, these writings reflected the influence of the 1930s, but usually they were indebted to forces set in motion by the civil rights movement of the 1950s. In addition, there was "history in the making" in unprecedented resistance to the war by ordinary citizens, as well as by those facing induction, such as Martin Jezer, quoted above. About one-third of the five hundred thousand individuals who applied for a conscientious objector classification, including thousands already in uniform, received them; while an estimated six hundred thousand men evaded the draft illegally, with thirty thousand to fifty thousand fleeing to Canada, and another twenty thousand fleeing to other countries or living underground in the United States.[2]

Although few writers critical of the Vietnam War were pacifists—many, in fact, were veterans, as Walter Lowenfels pointed out in 1967—the horrors of that war and the rationale responsible for it led many to condemn the violence outright.[3] The poems, novels, and essays went beyond mere polemic, "mere rhetoric"; as verbal creations, they indicated not only "what living feels like" but also "what it could be."

During these years, political theorists, such as Hannah Arendt, and strategists, such as Gene Sharp, were also attending to the implications of nonviolent campaigns in the United States and around the globe, and social scientists, particularly Kenneth Boulding, gave increasing attention to methods of building and maintaining "peace" in a cold-war world.

That is, while activists initiated nonviolent campaigns for civil rights in the South and for itinerant farm workers in the West, and against the war in Vietnam everywhere, a community of scholars endeavored to make theoretical sense out of these "experiments with truth" and to suggest their implications for the future. Their "peace research" centered, initially, on methods of resolving conflict nonviolently. In 1957, Boulding, an economist, and Herbert Kelman, a psychologist, launched *The Journal of Conflict Resolution* at the University of Michigan; and in 1964, shortly after the first meeting of the International Peace Research Association in Groningen, the Netherlands, Alan and Hannah Newcombe founded the *Journal of Peace Research*.

"Shivering American liberals, pacifists and internationalists [who] found few coals of comfort," as one historian put it, began to explore the possibilities of using "the quantitative, technical tools that had produced a system that seemed bent on destruction"; their goal was to transform it, so that it might work for the world's benefit.[4] Together with his wife, Elise Boulding, a sociologist, and their associates from this country and abroad, Kenneth Boulding provided a theoretical and organizational framework for peace research, including nonviolence. Others cooperating in that effort included Johan Galtung, a mathematician and sociologist who initiated the Peace Research Institute (Oslo), and Anatol Rappaport, a psychologist at the University of Toronto. Shortly afterward, Gene Sharp's major treatise, *The Politics of Nonviolent Action* (1973), offered theoretical concepts and analytical tools for studying nonviolent movements in various historical periods and cultural settings.

Even before the United States finally withdrew from Vietnam in 1975, peace activists began to shift their emphasis from that war to broader issues relating to military and economic priorities that made future "Vietnams" inevitable. In what may be regarded as the first academic "breakthrough" of the cold war, small colleges associated with traditional peace churches (Manchester and Goshen in Indiana; Haverford and Swarthmore colleges in Philadelphia), as well as Manhattan College, Colgate, and Syracuse universities, initiated courses and programs in peace and conflict studies. During the 1980s, responding to student concerns, fears, and anxieties associated with Reagan's nuclear buildup, even "empire schools" dependent upon and inevitably corrupted by Pentagon contacts and contracts (University of Wisconsin, Madison, for example) began to offer seminars and courses "studying peace."

The need to "rethink" matters related to conflict and mediation had been dramatized by radical increases in the manufacture and deployment of nuclear weapons. Since 1955, the psychological implications of nuclear war had fallen like a dark shadow over literature of the postmodernist period. In a prose poem by David Ignatow (b. 1914), for example, the speaker dreams of the funeral of the world, "watching it go by carried in an urn, reduced to ashes, and followed by a horde of mourners, a million abreast, across the broadest land and chanting together, We are dead, we have killed ourselves. We are beyond rescue."[5]

Anthologies of poetry and fiction, including work by the best writers in the language, focused upon "not just the fall of another empire, but of civilization and all of life itself," in the words of the editor of *Nuke-Rebuke: Writers and Artists Against Nuclear Energy & Weapons* (1984). Gradually, an alliance of sorts emerged among literary artists and social scientists, as they came to understand the effects of an "undeclared" nuclear war on children and adults. Their important findings appeared first in publications associated with nongovernmental agencies—Union of Concerned Scientists, International Physicians Against Nuclear War, and PEN, an association of Poets, Essayists and Novelists—then later in congressional hearings and the popular media.

"The bomb," psychologists and biologists noted, damaged psyches and destroyed resources long before it fell. It corrupted values and redirected foreign policy simply by its threatening presence, as an instrument of intimidation by imperial nations against smaller, poorer countries. A whole new vocabulary, words and phrases describing "the casualties," emerged to account for the effects of an undeclared "nuclear war."

Robert Jay Lifton, a child psychiatrist at Yale University, for example, talked about "psychic numbing"; that is, the paralyzing effect of the nuclear threat, including people's inability to name and thus to confront the fears that governed their lives. *In a Dark Time* (1984), which Lifton coedited, took its title from a lyric poem by Theodore Roethke written thirty years before; in the anthology, speakers in prose and poetry provided contrasting images of human beings as warriors or as victims and dupes of "Nukespeak" and, conversely, as resisters, saying "NO! in thunder," while endeavoring to regain control of their fate.

Religious and academic institutions were slow to respond to the nuclear crisis, though during the Vietnam era, some denominations—not just the traditional peace churches—issued statements supporting conscientious objection as an alternative to military service. And gradually, theologians and social philosophers began to question the possibility of anyone waging a "just" war with modern weapons.

By the late 1960s, writers whom one might least expect to do so acknowledged, even if they could not commend, the power of nonviolence in the effort to end the Indochina war. Among the most surprising tributes to nonviolent activists appeared in a novel by Norman Mailer (b. 1923), a writer long associated with the clichés of macho, Hemingway-esque social Darwinism. His *Armies of the Night: Novel as History, History as Novel* (1968) focused on the 1967 march on Washington, involving several well-known poets and novelists, including Robert Lowell and Mitchell Goodman, as well as journalists and social critics. Before the march, Lowell had turned down President Lyndon Johnson's invitation to a White House Arts Festival, as a protest against his war policies; in a carefully written, even courteous letter, Lowell warned that the administration's behavior put the United States in grave moral danger.

Those at the head of the march, in all the photographs and journalistic accounts, amounted to a kind of "who's who" of American intellectual life: Mailer, Lowell, Noam Chomsky, Dwight MacDonald, and Sidney Lens among them. But the authentic leadership was a small group of Quakers and members of the Committee for Nonviolent Action, who refused to cooperate in any way with the authorities and ended up in Occoquan, Virginia, and other jails.

The first two-thirds of Mailer's novel/memoir is a detailed, third-person journal, beginning with press reports of his uneasy sense of himself, his unexpected participation in events, his arrest and brief imprisonment. The next section concentrates on the witness, the crucial and dominating presence, of radical pacifists and Christian anarchists, and attempts "to elucidate the mysterious character of that quintessential American event" by paying tribute to the activists, as well as to the tradition they represent. In the last section, Mailer speaks of his own momentary "conversion," one might say, to nonviolence, among those who lived "for many days naked with blankets and mattresses on the floor. For many days they did not eat nor drink water."

"Who was to say they were not saints?" Mailer asks, in the powerful concluding sentences of the novel, "And who is to say that the sins of America were not by their witness a tithe remitted?" Bringing Mailer to this language is something of an achievement in itself, for these "unknown" nonviolent activists—Irene Johnson, Gary Rader, Suzanne Moore, Diane Enzer, among them:

> Here was the last of the rite of passage, "the chinook salmon . . . nosing up the impossible stone," here was the thin source of the stream—these naked Quakers on the cold floor of a dark isolation cell in D.C. jail, wandering down the hours in the fever of dehydration, the cells of the brain contracting to the crystals of their thought, essence of one thought so close to the essence of another—all separations of water gone—that madness is near, madness can now be no more than the acceleration of thought.[6]

Over the next few years, this small group, accelerated by "madness of thought," grew to a national network of activists, organizations, and publications committed to ending the war and to initiating campaigns for social change, with attendant effects on the literature of the postmodernist period.

In speaking of the Quakers' "madness," a pattern of thought preferable to "sanity," Mailer resorted to language similar to Ginsberg's, in *Howl*, a decade earlier, in taking the reader across a nuclear landscape ruled by the ancient, destructive god, Moloch. Theodore Roethke's "In a Dark Time"—often regarded as the period's greatest lyric poem—had defined madness, similarly, as "nobility of soul / At odds with circumstance." In fiction, discussions of "who is sane, who insane" informed several important and popular novels, including Joseph Heller's *Catch-22* (1961), discussed previously, and Kurt Vonnegut's *Slaughterhouse Five: The Children's Crusade—A Duty-Dance with Death* (1968). On the title page, the author describes himself as "a fourth-generation German-American now living in easy circumstances on Cape Cod (and smoking too much), who, as an American infantry scout *hors de combat,* as a prisoner of war, witnessed the fire-bombing of Dresden, Germany, 'the Florence of the Elbe.' " Surviving to tell the tale, the narrator writes just two nights after Robert Kennedy and one month after Martin Luther King Jr. was shot in 1968; he tells his sons that under no circumstances are they "to take part in massacres" or "to work for companies which make massacre machinery."

The "disintegration" of sanity described in literature continued—as another poet, Daniel Hoffman, said—amid the rubble of war in Korea and Indochina; the bureaucratization of the military-industrial-university complex; the exposure and disgrace of the Nixon presidency; the radical increase in war production under Reagan; and subsequent U.S. military intervention in Latin America and the Middle East.[7]

Robert Bly's "Asian Peace Offers Rejected Without Publication" (1967) spoke about mass insanity in the highest offices of government, accompanied by "a new corruption of language." Powerful men in Washington, D.C., the poem says, "are not men only—/ They are bombs waiting to be loaded in a darkened hangar."

> Longing to get back to their offices
> So they can cling to the underside of the steel wings
> shuddering faintly in the high altitudes.

In the next stanza, the poem links this scene, reminiscent of Billy Wilder's black comedy, *Dr. Strangelove; or How I Learned to Stop Worrying and Love the Bomb,* and the American West, where "Lost angels huddled on a night branch!" and where

> something inside us
> Like a ghost train in the Rockies
> About to be buried in snow![8]

In "Declaration of Independence from the War in Vietnam," written the same year, Martin Luther King Jr. called his "own government . . . the greatest purveyor of violence in the world today."

The writings of activists and poets, in other words, echoed and complemented one another, as both groups supported and built small communities of resistance. In 1965, Robert Bly and David Ray had initiated an organization called Poets Against the War in Vietnam, which sponsored readings and forums on campuses throughout the country to benefit draft resisters and others committed to nonviolent direct action. And when he received the National Book Award for *The Light Around the Body,* on March 6, 1968, Bly chided the awards committee for inviting "as a speaker Vice-President Humphrey, famous for his lies," then gave the one-thousand-dollar award to the resistance and urged young men "to defy the draft authorities—and not to destroy their spiritual lives by participating in this war."

Although Bly's poetry lost much of its vigor and particularity when he later donned the mantle as guru of the so-called men's movement, he continued to speak out as a citizen against U.S. intervention abroad. Arrested as part of an extended campaign against Honeywell's weapons industry, Bly spoke out against the Persian Gulf War, as well. In February 1991, in an essay using Randolph Bourne's famous epithet of 1917, "War Is the Health of the State," Bly called George Bush's "manic adventure" against Iraq "the greatest mistake ever made by an American president."[9]

Through his poetry, an award-winning play, *The Trial of the Catonsville Nine,* and numerous interviews, essays, and religious writings, Daniel Berrigan (b. 1921)—like Bly, a Minnesota native—was an influential figure as nonviolent activist and writer, particularly among the Catholic community. Following the death of his friend, fellow priest and writer Thomas Merton, in 1968, Berrigan became, in quite a different way, one of the country's major voices for active resistance to government-sponsored killing.

Arrested with his brother Philip, the artist Tom Lewis, former Maryknoll missionaries Tom and Marjorie Melville, and others for burning draft files at Catonsville, Maryland, on May 17, 1968, Daniel Berrigan spent several months underground, pursued by a frustrated and embarrassed Federal Bureau of Investigation, and two years in Danbury Federal Prison. His play, *The Trial of the Catonsville Nine,* based upon his trial, used "factual theater," in the manner of contemporary French drama. It interspersed court testimony about the crimes of the Vietnam War by those on trial for burning draft files with relevant quotations from earlier social critics and literary radicals: Jean Paul Sartre, Albert Camus, Pablo Neruda, Bertolt Brecht, and C. Wright Mills. The play—successful on Broadway, translated into forty languages, performed throughout the world, and made into a film—carried the message of nonviolent resistance to a wide audience. Many people who would not listen to critics of America's armed intervention in far-off countries were drawn to the simple testimony of "ordinary people" such as John Hogan, Mary Moylan, and George Mische, and to their moral indictment of the U.S. government, at the heart of the drama.

Among various poems of the same period, "Skunk," by Daniel Berrigan, is a successful and witty "manifesto" about saying no to injustice and violence. The engaging, humane speaker salutes a skunk as it wanders into the yard at Danbury Federal Prison, during the period of Berrigan's incarceration there. And although Berrigan and his cellmates "didn't want additional / prisoners, even dumb ones,"

> If they must come, atavistic,
> mystical, then let them be
> spectaculars, trouble-
> shooters. O skunk, raise
> against lawnorder, your grandiose
> geysering stinking *NO!*[10]

The voice speaking, at once serious and satiric, is that of someone whose commitment to nonviolence has become as elemental as bone marrow.

Since the late 1960s, Daniel and his younger brother Philip have gone to jail repeatedly rather than remain silent about war crimes and the threat of nuclear annihilation. Such persistent witness inevitably brought them into conflict with the institutional church complicit in these policies. Soon after they helped to initiate the first "peace movement" among American Catholics—as cofounders of the Catholic Peace Fellowship and of Clergy and Laity Concerned About Vietnam, for example—Daniel was exiled to South America by Francis Spellman, then Cardinal/Archbishop of New York. Berrigan returned home shortly, after a public outcry, more committed than ever to "divine disobedience," as he called it. About the same time, Philip, also a priest—that is, before he left to marry Elizabeth McAlister—was dismissed from the seminary run by his religious order, the Josephites, in Newburgh, New York, and was stationed in Baltimore.

In spite of "dungeon, fire, and sword," the Berrigans have persisted, all the while developing new strategies for exposing injustice and resisting the warmaking state. In 1980, they helped to initiate a group called Plowshares and a series of "direct actions" at nuclear weapons plants and missile bases, "disarming" them and pouring blood over them. These activities and the public trials that followed involved scholars, public officials, and well-known scientists—former attorney general Ramsey Clark, Howard Zinn, Robert Jay Lifton, Richard Falk—as expert witnesses on behalf of the defendants, and sent several people, particularly Helen Woodson and Carl Kabat, a priest, into federal prison for many years. Their campaign, the work of several communities, led to several new periodicals, including *Year One* and *Catholic Radical*, as well as anthologies of essays and poems. In a representative later manifesto, "JUBILEE" (1989), marking his fifty years as a Jesuit, Daniel Berrigan indicated that his commitment remains strong after three decades:

> A fairly modest urging—
> Don't kill for whatever pretext.
> Leave the world unbefouled.
> Don't hoard. Stand somewhere.

The militant and religious "ultra resistance" associated with the burning of draft files signified a new direction for the peace movement in 1968. Although that "escalation"—that is, the destruction of property—evoked violent responses in some quarters (the Weathermen's bombing of chemical labs and the Progressive Labor Party's trashing of bank windows during demonstrations), the commitment to nonviolence deepened among the small community that had initiated the antiwar movement in 1964–65. This was particularly true among traditional pacifist organizations, the War Resisters League, the Community for Creative Nonviolence, Fellowship of Reconciliation, and American Friends Service Committee.

And although some nonviolent activists have tolerated individual acts of violence as a means of provoking change, the Berrigans, during the Vietnam War, as well as with the later Plowshares, restrict themselves to the destruction of property, never people. In "Guns Don't Work," Daniel Berrigan described that commitment much as his "nonviolent ancestor," Elihu Burritt, had in 1854: *"No political change is worth . . . a single drop of human blood!"*. Or as Berrigan put it, in an open letter to fellow poet and priest Ernesto Cardenal: "The death of a single human is too heavy a price to pay for the vindication of any principle, however sacred." The practical and strategic meaning of this commitment includes refusing "to take up bombs or guns, aimed at the flesh of brothers and sisters, whom we persist in defining as such"; and "refusing the enmities pushed at us by war-making state or war-blessing church."[11]

The Catholic Worker movement, which had nurtured writers and artists since its founding in 1933, accounted for a significant body of work associated with traditional and new nonviolent initiatives. Pacifist and anarchist in its politics, with links to earlier American radicalism, *The Catholic Worker* published essays and poems by Thomas Merton, Daniel Berrigan, and Denise Levertov, among others. Performers and street theater activists—Ed Sanders, Tuli Kupferberg, and the Fugs (mentioned earlier)—acknowledged an indebtedness to the *Catholic Worker,* as well, and Abbie Hoffman spoke repeatedly of his admiration for Dorothy Day.

Among literary and historical documents associated with the Catholic Worker movement, Jack Cook's *Rags of Time: A Season in Prison* (1972), the story of an anarchist walk by draft resisters at Allenwood (Pa.) Federal Prison, is a particularly important contribution to the nonviolent tradition. Although it belongs to the genre of prison literature, including the memoirs of Alexander Berkman, Eugene Victor Debs, and Ammon Hennacy, *Rags of Time* unites the history of dissent and nonviolence in a special way, with similarities to Eldridge Cleaver's *Soul on Ice* (1970).

Taking his title from John Donne's "Sun Rising," Cook provides a convincing dramatization of nonviolence in action, focusing on his twenty-three months in jail, after refusing induction into the army, in one telling episode: a brief walk "from the inside" by prison inmates at Lewisburg (Pa.) Federal Prison to support an antiwar demonstration outside the gates. In describing events, Cook "telescopes" time. Much in the manner of Thoreau, who went to Walden Pond "to live deliberately, to front only the essential facts of life," Cook forces life into a corner and finds more truth there than many find in "the mess" outside.

Cook and his associates regard their walk toward the gate and the demonstrators—to some a meaningless gesture or "pipe dream"—as a means of reclaiming themselves in a dark time. And for a few brief moments, amid the anonymity and hopelessness of prison, they get that "vague sense," a renewed vision of love, freedom, peace. "We who are concerned more with undermining than founding a state, more with the transforming of people into persons than with the reforming of institutions; more with values and principles than with laws and rules of conduct; more with love as letting be than with love as making by force you into me—we should foster pipe dreams where we find them, make them come true if we can."

Eventually thrown into "the hole," Cook and others imprisoned for conscience's sake suffered solitary confinement for their protest: a cell six feet by nine feet, with sewer bugs and flies, bare feet sticking to the filthy floor, heavy iron clanging doors, total isolation from friends and the sound of natural human voices. Even there, under conditions resembling those in Dostoevsky's or Solzhenitsyn's Siberian prisons—yet close by, in a Mid-Atlantic state in 1970—the resisters make "bad time" into "good," and celebrate their release in a kind of ecstatic state. "Jailed for breaking laws of the state, we break the laws of the jail," Cook says. "Proving we are still free even in fetters. As all men should be. And without blame. Without blame."[12]

Cook's chronicle of a truly "nonviolent" action, a gesture of reconciliation, "ourselves with each other, ourselves with ourselves" is special for any time, but particularly for the time in which it was written, the latter days of the Vietnam period, when antiwar literature became strident, preachy, sometimes one-dimensional. By 1970, the hope of ending the war had been undermined, not to say betrayed, by the Nixon administration. And the frustration of activists against the war—exacerbated, undoubtedly, by the murder of Martin Luther King Jr. and Robert Kennedy in 1968—exhibited itself in the divisions, animosities, "bad" art, and politics of the movement.

Antiwar poems, in this period, came to reflect the alienation, violence, and hate of a generation in despair. In an anthology, *Campfires of the*

Resistance: Poetry from the Movement, with a burning streetsign on the cover, a poem by Robert Mezey, "How Much Longer," said, "War is in everyone's eyes, war is made / in the kitchen, in the bedroom, in the car at stoplights." Fewer people in the larger movement spoke of conflict resolution or reconciliation, and the war went on.

Similarly, a poem by Marge Piercy, "The Peaceable Kingdom," using the same title that Edward Hicks gave to his eighteenth-century painting, sounded more like a poem about the end of the world than about Isaiah's utopian vision of peace. Another Piercy poem, "Community," began with this line: "Loving feels lonely in a violent world."[13] Even Denise Levertov, who usually retained a sense of the sacredness of life and the possibilities of peace, began to sound rhetorical and, occasionally, self-satisfied, in a country divided between "good guys and bad guys."

Not long after the end of the Indochina war in 1975, war-weary citizens embraced or at least tolerated the complacent, then cruel years of Reagan and Bush. Meanwhile, writers continued to address the pervasive violence of America's domestic and foreign policy. They wrote precisely, less sarcastically than before, about Reagan's nuclear buildup and American imperialism. Previously reactive, emphasizing an antiwar theme (or what Kenneth Boulding calls "negative peace"), poets and novelists found a language to speak convincingly about efforts to imagine and then to construct "positive peace." In doing so, they used images, language, and concepts long associated with the history of nonviolence, speaking a "language of peace," as Denise Levertov said in "Making Peace" (1983), rather than merely criticizing, while still echoing, the "language of war."

Speaking to this condition, Wendell Berry (b. 1934) had earlier written a kind of epitaph to antiwar poems, "The Morning's News." Poet, essayist, and fiction writer long concerned with environmental—or perhaps more accurately, pastoral—issues, Berry focused on a persistent postmodernist theme, that is, the conflict between poet and state. Sickened by the human race's "complicity" in killing, he compared man, "the inventor of cold violence," unfavorably with other creatures:

> To kill in hot savagery like a beast
> is understandable. It is forgivable and curable.
> But to kill by design, deliberately, without wrath,
> that is the sullen labor that perfects Hell.

Eventually, the speaker in the poem faces a choice similar to the one faced by pacifists, conscientious objectors, and Christian anarchists over the centuries:

What must I do
to go free? I think I must put on
a deathlier knowledge, and prepare to die
rather than enter into the design of man's hate.

Not an easy or popular choice, it nonetheless enables a person and the heart to remain "faithful to a mystery in a cloud," as "the summer's garden continues its descent / through me, toward the ground."[14] For Berry, "our hatred of the world is most insidiously and dangerously present in the constantly widening discrepancy between our power and our needs, our means and our ends." Searching for peaceful alternatives, he focused on the seamless web of creation and the wisdom of personal and local efforts, rather than campaigns and abstractions about a global order, in his effort to "save this planet."

In literature associated with nonviolent social change in this period, the work of three poets "modeled" what a language of peace might sound like: Muriel Rukeyser (1913–1980), William Stafford, and Denise Levertov (b. 1923). In that special company—and for other reasons as well —the writings of Rukeyser deserve a special place.

Although less well-known among readers, perhaps, than other writers discussed here, Rukeyser is, I think, among the most essential, original, and powerful poets in American literature. Respected, even praised, by her peers—particularly Levertov and Adrienne Rich—Rukeyser was seldom read seriously, that is, approved of, by influential literary critics. Like other writers deeply involved in the political turmoil of their time— Milton, Defoe, Blake, Shelley, Pound, and Orwell—she often changed styles or direction at the precise moment that other modes of writing became the fashion.

In 1945, for example, just as the New Criticism was in the ascendancy, Rukeyser moved from New York to California and began preparing the way for the eventual San Francisco Renaissance of the 1950s; similarly, in 1970, when American poetry fell under the influence of "open form," she returned to regular verse patterns and to rhyme, including the ballad stanza. Perhaps for that reason, her writings, as well as her life, provide valuable insights into the relationship between resistance and creativity at the heart of nonviolence. "I will protest all my life," Rukeyser once said, "I am willing to. But I'm a person who makes, much more than a person who protests . . . and I have decided that wherever I protest from now on, . . . I will make something—I will make poems, plant, feed children, build, but not ever protest without making something."[15]

Rukeyser's "voice" was the voice of those victimized by poverty and war, from her careful documentary poems about unemployed miners during the Great Depression to on-site portraits of events during the Spanish civil war; from her peace mission to North Vietnam in the 1960s to her later interventions on behalf of the Korean poet Kim Chi-Ha, imprisoned and sentenced to death in Seoul.

Her "Poem," beginning "I lived in the first century of world war" (1970), makes some essential distinctions between the "language of war" and the "language of peace." It provides a useful reference point regarding a shift in emphasis in American poetry and powerful insights into what living a nonviolent ethic requires in this violent century. After describing the psychological effect of "the first century of world war" on all of us, "Poem" moves to a simple, direct statement about "making peace" in a time of perpetual war. As with Gandhi and King, Rukeyser argues—though less rhetorically than they—that a just social order begins with a revolution of the heart, a reformation from within. Thinking of them, the speaker in "Poem" remembers

> men and women
> Brave, setting up signals across vast distances,
> Considering a nameless way of living, of almost unimagined values.

Though public in its implications, peacemaking, as the poem says, begins with simple, personal daily acts, as each of us endeavors

> To construct peace, to make love, to reconcile
> Waking with sleeping, ourselves with each other,
> Ourselves with ourselves. We would try by any means
> To reach the limits of ourselves, to reach beyond
>   ourselves,
> To let go the means, to wake.

> I lived in the first century of these wars.[16]

By the late 1960s, when "Poem" was written, Rukeyser had a thirty-year history of involvement with movements for social change. Bloody but unbowed, having survived conflicting and messy ideological struggles since the 1930s, she spoke modestly but clearly about the injustices of her time.

The daughter of a wealthy Philadelphia family, Rukeyser had been influenced by libertarian ideas and ideals among Jewish intellectuals in

New York, where she grew up and attended a progressive high school. As a student at Vassar College, where she was a contemporary of Mary Mc-Carthy and Elizabeth Bishop, she had come to the defense of the Scottsboro Boys, nine black youths unjustly accused of rape, in a famous trial in Alabama in the early 1930s; traveling south to cover the trial, she even served a brief period in jail when she refused to follow a court order not to report on the trial. During the "radical decade" and subsequently, she wrote a number of extraordinary poems about workers organizing in the United States, the struggle against fascism in Spain, and the responsibility to resist the inanities of a cruel century.

Another of her major poems, written during World War II and in a sequence called "Letter to the Front," suggests her lifelong effort to understand the centrality of conflict in human affairs, personal and social. Rejecting conflict is, at some level, she argues, a rejection of life itself—and perhaps of one's destiny as a human being.

> To be a Jew in the twentieth century
> Is to be offered a gift. If you refuse,
> Wishing to be invisible, you choose
> Death of the spirit, the stone insanity.[17]

Throughout her life and work, Rukeyser returned to this central theme in poetry that provides one of the richest sources of insight into nonviolence available in imaginative literature.

Rukeyser's knowledge about and meditation on how to resolve conflict, and thus to de-escalate violence, came from her awareness of herself as a woman. And in poems such as "Effort at Speech Between Two People," "More of a Corpse Than a Woman," "Myth," and especially " 'Long Enough,' " she conveys the sense of struggle as she resisted humiliation and sexual discrimination in a world dominated by men. In tracing this journey, she provided a vivid sense, in appropriate language, of personal and social conflicts associated with sexual politics and a patriarchal system:

> "Long enough, Long enough,"
> I heard a woman say—
> I am that woman who too long
> Under the web lay.
> Long enough in the empire
> Of his blackened eyes
> Bewildered in the greying silver
> Light of his fantasies.

Recognizing the erotic implications of a handsome man's hold on her attention ("the empire"), she refuses to remain captive to his fantasies. In the conclusion, she moves to

> Walk out of the pudorweb
> And into a lifetime
> . . . and I sleeper began to wake
> And to say my own name.[18]

Rukeyser declared herself, and took a stand, without resorting to bitterness or cynicism, attitudes that often accompany feelings of victimization and domination.

Although they are obviously more than that, Rukeyser's poems are the record of a lifelong effort to resolve potentially violent conflicts in her own life and to dramatize the inevitable relationship between inner and outer peace. Even in her second to last book, *Breaking Open* (1973), she continues to document her resolution to address everyday conflict and confusion, in precise and original language.

"Ballad of Orange and Grape," for example, describes, with extraordinary wit, a condition of "unstable peace," to use Kenneth Boulding's term, and the difficulty of achieving "stable peace." "On a blistering afternoon in East Harlem in the twentieth century," the speaker watches a waiter in a hot dog stand pouring

> bright purple in the one marked ORANGE
> orange in the one marked GRAPE
> pouring orange drink into the machine marked ORANGE
> and orange drink in the GRAPE.

"It could be violence and nonviolence," the poem continues, white and black, women and men,

> war or peace or any
> binary system, love and hate, enemy, friend.
> Yes and no, be and not-be, what we do and what we don't do.[19]

In another poem, Rukeyser described the persistence, the discipline, that "making peace" requires not only in the public order but also in private lives, during this "first century of world war":

Waking this morning,
a violent woman in the violent day
Laughing. . . . I want strong peace, and
     delight,
the wild good.
I want to make my touch poems:
to find my morning, to find you entire,
alive among the anti-touch people.
          I say across the waves of the air to you
today once more
I will try to be non-violent
one more day
this morning, waking the world away
in the violent day.[20]

And finally, in "It Is There," she provided, for the language of her time, a positive image/sound/argument of peace:

the city full of music,
Flute music, sounds of children, voices of poets,
The unknown bird in his long call.

Characterized as action rather than inaction, as sound rather than silence, peace

sounds across the water
In the long parks where the lovers are walking
Along the lake with its island and pagoda. . . .
          Meditation, yes; but within a tension
Of long resistance to all invasion,
          all seduction of hate.
Generations of holding to resistance;
          and within this resistance
Fluid change that can respond,
          that can show the children
A long future of finding, of responsibility;[21]

Since at least the seventeenth century, most notably in the work of George Herbert (1593–1633), poets in English had been trying, with limited success, to suggest the positive nature, not to say the "power" of peace, in words and images. In this poem, and in others, Rukeyser managed not only to suggest the tenor of peace but also to describe the complex integration of inner and outer worlds that might bring it into being.

In a similar way, William Stafford wrote a number of poems significant in the literature, suggesting the perpetual "struggle" associated with resistance to violence and war, as well as the tenor and character of "positive peace." (The same is true of his prose memoir, *Down in My Heart*, discussed earlier.) "Meditation," an eight-line verse, for example, provides almost a metaphysics of the inevitability of violence and the essential human task of peacemaking, with God depending upon his creatures to heal an incomplete and injured world:

> Animals full of light
> walk through the forest
> toward someone aiming a gun
> loaded with darkness.
>
> That's the world: God
> holding still
> letting it happen,
> and again and again.[22]

In interviews, Stafford occasionally acknowledged a link between his commitment to pacifism and his writing, his attitude toward conflict and the larger world. "My impulse, even in protest," he once said, "is toward some kind of redemptive move toward the opposition," echoing the statement of Martin Luther King Jr. about forgiveness being "not merely an attitude, but a way of life." The building of community is also a recurring theme, as in his poem "Smoke Signals," about the subtle, affirming sense of people working toward a common goal, even when they are not directly associated with one another:

> Something about how they have accepted
> their lives, or how the sunlight happens to them,
> helps us to hold the strange, enigmatic days
> in line for our own living . . .
> here is a smoke
> signal, unmistakable but unobtrusive—we are
> following what comes, going through the world
> knowing each other, building our little fires.[23]

In one of his later poems, "Globescope," Stafford focuses on "world citizenship" or what Richard Falk might call "globalization-from-below" (see chap. 7). It is a concept that nonviolent activists and strategists, from Thomas Paine to Jane Addams, have been concerned with for centuries.

Not surprisingly, Stafford chooses that most accessible of all democratic images, from the title of Whitman's collected poems, *Leaves of Grass,* as his global symbol. "Grass is our flag," says the poem, which whispers,

> "Asia,
> Asia, Dakota, Dakota, Prairie, Steppe."
> All over the world it leans above rivers— . . .
> It is a good flag. But sometimes others
> hover above and all around us,
> relying on some great Beowulf satellite
> infallibly orbited, loaded with warheads,
> patrolling, lashing a laser and ready
> against all enemies.

Against the heavy weight of policies and warriors, ordinary people make a pledge of their lives,

> whatever happens, we are faithful
> in that world story where the rivers flow
> and the wind discovers its great following,
> and the grass whispers.[24]

The conflict between war and peace has been a preoccupation for some time, and the work of Denise Levertov covers a wide range of additional subjects and themes: mythology, love—both eros and agape— social protest, nature, the city. Her poems successfully combine personal and social concerns, private life and public issues that have informed the best literature by recent American writers; often, also, they speak with particular authority and conviction about various ways of working toward positive peace.

Our condition since 1945, after all, has been unique, not only as citizens of a young republic but also as a major imperial power. That power, as it dominated so much else in its path, overwhelmed the culture; it influences and alters the food we eat, the diseases we suffer, the clothes we wear, the educational and political structures we build and tolerate, complain about, and resist. Meanwhile, the security we so vainly tried to achieve by force of arms, particularly in the 1980s, constantly eluded us— and as our military strength approached infinity, our security approached zero.

Underlying all our hopes and fears, as psychiatrists indicated, was an elemental anxiety about an all-encompassing war. In her poem "Life at

War," Levertov spoke of that perpetual twentieth-century war, beginning in 1914; it continued through the 1940s, spreading then across the Middle East, Central America, Southeast Asia, Eastern Europe, to wherever the morning headlines heralded its new arrival. "My heart . . . could I say of it, it overflows / with bitterness," Levertov says, quoting Rainer Maria Rilke, then adding, "The same war / continues."[25]

In a companion poem, written fifteen years after "Life at War," Levertov argued for structures that might enable us to live at peace, without minimizing the hard work, the personal sacrifice required for radical social change. Among the poem's accomplishments in language and tone is its success in conveying that peace is not "soft" but "hard," perhaps even harder than war, and in setting down the proper conditions of achieving it.

> A line of peace might appear
> if we restructured the sentence our lives are making,
> revoked its reaffirmation of profit and power,
> questioned our needs, allowed
> long pauses. . . .[26]

In life, as in art, "Making Peace" concludes, the time has come for a revaluation of values. In this effort is our hope for a new society, including an appropriate language for mediation. To sustain this vision, Levertov agrees with the suggestion spoken by the piece of sculpture in Rilke's poem "Archaic Torso of Apollo": "You must change your life."

In an effort to encourage reform, Levertov believes, as Orwell said in "Politics and the English Language," that "one ought to recognize that the present political chaos is connected with the decay of language, and that one can probably bring about some improvement by starting at the verbal end." And so nonviolent resistance to injustice and humiliation begins with telling the truth, whatever the consequences. No wonder that, in struggles for peace and justice in the former Soviet Union (Mandelstam), South Korea (Kim Chi-Ha), the United States (Rukeyser, Berrigan, Ginsberg, Bly), and elsewhere, poets were among the first citizens and protesters to wind up in prison. During the Indochina war, a number of them followed the example of nineteenth-century American writers (Bronson Alcott and Thoreau) who went to jail at the time of the Mexican War, in advocating tax resistance against the whole war system.

Among younger poets, including those who came of age during the Vietnam War, the work of cataloging the horrors and memories of successive wars, as well as the inherent violence of the cold war, continued.

Bruce Weigl (b. 1949), in *Song of Napalm* (1988), for example, spoke about the wounded who remain casualties of the war long after it ended. In a poem reminiscent of Wilfred Owen's "Disabled," describing a veterans' hospital after the First World War, Weigl wrote, as if "on location," about a Vietnam veteran haunted by

> the girl
> running from her village, napalm
> stuck to her dress like jelly,
> her hand reaching for the no one
> who waits in waves of heat before her.

Returning home, the soldier later confesses to his young wife that

> Nothing
> can change that, she is burned behind my eyes
> and not your good love and not the rain-swept air
> and not the jungle's green
> pasture unfolding before us can deny it.[27]

Haunted by such memories, young veterans faced only more talk of war and more foreign interventions over the next twenty years and into the 1990s, in Lebanon, Grenada, Panama, the Persian Gulf.

Amid the violence of the status quo, activists and writers remained painfully aware that their efforts to recommend nonviolent alternatives were inevitably tentative, modest, and only partly "successful." Marge Piercy's poem "The 14th Demonstration," for example, described the experimental nature of nonviolent resistance and the fragile nature of new communities associated with it. The poem concludes on a sardonic, though witty, note regarding the predictability of protest marches. Someone asks, "Tomorrow is the 15th Demonstration / Will you be there?" "Of course," the speaker answers.[28]

Through the 1970s and 1980s, the despair that many felt after the assassinations of Malcolm X, Robert Kennedy, Martin Luther King Jr., and the death of Thomas Merton, haunted the literature of that period, as domestic violence, the nuclear arms race, and military interventions abroad increased. During the Reagan/Bush years, D. H. Lawrence's statement about the inherent "killer instinct" of American culture took on new meaning; it seemed, as Piercy said at one point, a nation "founded on blood like a city on swamps . . . as brutal and heavy as a burned out star." Yet, as Robert Bly had observed in "Those Being Eaten by America," in the midst of violence, "small communities of the saved" continued to call the nation to justice, to judgment. And in "About Political Action in Which Each Individual Acts from the Heart" (1982), Levertov noted modest, positive achievements among the resisters:

> when we taste in small victories sometimes
> the small, ephemeral yet joyful
> harvest of our striving,
> great power flows from us,
> luminous, a promise. Yes! . . . Then
>
> great energy flows from solitude,
> and great power from communion.[29]

There is little cause or room for triumphalism in the literature of nonviolence of this period, certainly few happy endings or final victories. In an imperial country, the literature of postmodernism argues that struggles for justice and peace never end—they must merely be taken up again by successive generations. Throughout the cold war years, nonetheless, these writers persisted, as pacifists and nonpacifists, ordinary and extraordinary people, and sustained, indeed enriched, a tradition now three hundred years old. Against all the odds, they continued to "say across the waves of the air,"

> today once more
> I will try to be non-violent
> one more day
> this morning, waking the world away
> in the violent day.

7

Against Forgetting
1990 and After

Global citizenship . . . rests upon the highly pragmatic conviction that what is currently taken to be realistic is not sustain-
able.

—Richard Falk[1]

$\mathbb{A}$bout 1990, American literature in
the nonviolent tradition began to reflect significant changes associated
with "a new world order," with important aesthetic and cultural implications for the future. Although not the dominant preoccupation of recent
writers—issues surrounding nonviolence seldom are—these "global visions" are consistent with the priorities and values associated with the
American tradition over three centuries. As citizens of one country flow
over into the next, activists and writers, without losing a sense of their
own locale, immerse themselves in the trials and misfortunes of refugees
across borders and cultures.

The story: Eight members of an extended family walk across the
desert of southwestern Arizona, having left Guatemala and El Salvador
several days before. They have traveled by crowded bus or car north into
Mexico, where they met guides (called coyotes), who took them through
barbed wire fences along the northern border, into the United States.
They had left home after being warned that their lives were in danger;
friends and relatives had been killed or had been carried away as conscripts
by soldiers trained in, and armed with weapons from, the United States.
The coyotes have abandoned them, so the eight are now on their own,
not sure their water supply will hold out. What they fear most is being

arrested as illegal aliens and returned to their country because returnees are seldom heard from again.

Three years later, in 1984, in a courtroom in Tucson, Jim Corbett, arrested and brought to trial for harboring these same political refugees, says to a judge: "From the Declaration of Independence to the trials at Nuremberg, our country has recognized that good citizenship requires that we disobey laws or officials whenever they mandate the violation of human rights. A government that commits crimes against humanity forfeits its claims to legitimacy."[2]

As a Quaker, Corbett had acted and now defended himself before the court much in the manner of his fellow religionists and other nonviolent activists since the seventeenth century. Like them, Corbett had initiated a modest effort, with a handful of people, to provide "justice and liberty for human beings whom many Americans considered less than equal."[3] In their active and practical response to a recent injustice, Corbett and his associates symbolized the resourcefulness of the nonviolent tradition and its periodical reemergence "into the light" in previous periods of American history. During the years between their initial efforts and the trial, the Sanctuary movement also rediscovered—and perhaps introduced new— strategies that indicated the power of a movement that reached beyond the United States to a larger, global community.

Elsewhere, about that time, a campaign coordinated by people trained in nonviolent direct action brought down the Marcos dictatorship in the Philippines; imaginative and courageous university students, joined by workers, exposed and challenged corruption, nepotism, and press censorship throughout China; ordinary people ended the rule of the ruling party, beginning with largescale, spontaneous nonviolent resistance to an attempted coup in the former Soviet Union; nonviolent demonstrations, made up mostly of university students, teachers, and townspeople, ousted a military regime in Thailand. Acts of resistance and reconciliation also extended the possibilities for democratic rule in some countries of Eastern Europe and South Korea.

By 1990, activists had begun to experiment with ever more daring and effective tactics of nonviolent intervention. And the communities supporting and sustaining these efforts continued to grow and develop, with connections to similar groups in many countries of the world, including a number of writers directly or indirectly involved in the struggles.

In the United States, the Plowshares actions, which began with eight people hammering the nose cone of an MX missile at the General Electric plant in King of Prussia, Pennsylvania, in 1980, numbered over fifty such "interventions" by 1994, at nuclear weapons plants and military bases in the United States, Germany, England, and Australia. In 1991, during the Persian Gulf War, teams of citizens from more than forty countries interposed themselves between the battle lines in Iraq in a nonviolent effort to stop the killing, and Peace Brigades International maintained a persistent presence in Sri Lanka as a way of supporting mediation between warring factions in that country. Along the Burmese-Thai border, Nobel peace laureates of several nationalities gathered in support of a compatriot, Aung San Suu Kyi, under house arrest in her native Burma. In 1993, the decade-long efforts of conflict resolution teams, working at every political level to de-escalate violence among Palestinians and Israelis, resulted in accords in the Middle East. During the ongoing civil war in the former Yugoslavia, We Share One Peace, made up of thousands of peacemakers from Italy, France, the United States, and other countries, risked their lives to bring direct aid to and to support reconciliation in Sarajevo and Mostar.

At the very moment when violence dominated news from every corner of the world—threatening and killing so many—modest, persistent, nonviolent initiatives increased.

Almost as surprising to anyone familiar with the academic wing of the military-industrial-university complex in the United States, "experts" in international affairs who once ignored or dismissed nonviolent initiatives as naïve were discussing proposals for nonviolent civilian defense and for maintaining national security. Smaller nations—Estonia, Latvia, Lithuania—watching the economic superpowers collapse under the weight of expenditures for nuclear fantasies and "star wars"—adopted nonviolent strategies for protecting themselves against potential aggressors.[4]

Although their efforts paled before the escalating violence of the international arms trade (the United States being the major supplier of armaments to the world) and of civil strife and drug wars at home, nonviolent activists and strategists introduced significant new factors in political debate, with important implications for the future. In the past, particularly throughout the cold war, questions of war and peace had been regarded primarily as the "domain" of political scientists and international relations specialists. Increasingly, however, scholars and researchers relied on insights accessible in a variety of academic disciplines—initially psychology, physics, and biology, then sociology, anthropology, religion, the arts. In a few universities, interdisciplinary peace studies encouraged systematic inquiries into long-neglected issues associated with human rights, international refugees, and ecology.

In addressing or resolving conflict, scholars and researchers began to use language that was "rational" rather than merely "objective," in Ursula Le Guin's useful distinction.[5] And even the language of diplomacy in international affairs began to sound more like the language of people than of committees. As before, notable literary works by American writers reflected and commented upon these initiatives, offering "diffused faint clews and indirections," as Whitman said of his poems, for the future. A central preoccupation of the nonviolent tradition, Paine's concept of being "a citizen of the world" and Garrison's of our "countrymen" being all humankind, had become a preoccupation of writers in various genres.

A significant moment for American literature was the appearance of two books, Miriam Davidson's narrative/memoir on the Sanctuary movement, mentioned above, and Carolyn Forche's anthology of poetry, a "poetry of witness," whose title I appropriated for this chapter.

Through memoir, which has long occupied a special place in American literature, writers remembered their history by extending and enriching the nonviolent tradition in a substantive manner. In *Convictions of the Heart: Jim Corbett and the Sanctuary Movement* (1988), for example, Davidson described small communities of support that sprang up, over several years, in the Sanctuary movement. Resembling the underground railways for African Americans at the time of slavery and for draft and war resisters during the Vietnam War, these new communities stretched along the Mexican border, from lower California to the Gulf, and from there to New England and Canada. Faith and energy sustained this ragtag ecumenical group and confirmed their belief "that violence solved nothing" and that "pacifism"—often characterized "as a copout, as fuzzy-headed utopianism, as pathetically naïve"—could be "at least as powerful and effective a weapon as violence."[6]

Davidson's book opens with a preface, "The Inner Light," about John Woolman, effectively dramatizing the obvious similarities between Woolman's effort to free slaves in New Jersey and Pennsylvania one century before the Civil War and Corbett's effort to free people "considered less than equal" on the other side of the continent 240 years later. Davidson records, in memoir fashion, events from July 5, 1980, through the famous trial of civil disobedients, October 1985 through May 1986, with a postscript on the historic peace treaty signed by Central American governments in Guatemala City in 1987.

In the intervening years, Corbett and others initiated a community that became a model for nonviolent resistance across various boundaries. "Sanctuary, in its broadest sense, extends far beyond Central America and specific human refugees to the need for harmonious community among all that lives."[7] In time, the Sanctuary movement led to other initiatives by nonviolent activists in the United States at the time of the Gulf War, the overthrow of Aristide in Haiti, and an internecine war in the former Yugoslavia.

Americans who provided sanctuary saw new connections between the military budget at home and government policies abroad, as a host of nongovernmental organizations emerged and developed. Innumerable ones were local; several were national—Neighbor to Neighbor, Citizens In Solidarity with the People of El Salvador; others reached, tentatively, toward indigenous movements abroad, particularly in Africa and South Asia. The literature associated with this movement dramatized "connections" that were also unprecedented. For example, the Sanctuary movement had emphasized the relationship between liberation theology, which revitalized the Catholic Church's commitment to justice in Latin America, and ecumenical coalitions, which sustained the peace movement in the United States.

Although the implications of this international movement for the future of the nonviolent tradition and American literature are uncertain, it is significant, perhaps, that the international literary scene, represented by the Nobel committee, awarded its annual prize to two women writers, Nadine Gordimer and Toni Morrison, whose stories and literary criticism specifically "make room" for previously ignored or silent presences. And the social structure—not to mention "the infrastructure"—of the United States and of other major economic powers increasingly reflects the volatile effects of large refugee populations.

Carolyn Forche's anthology *Against Forgetting*, gathering "works of poetic witness to the sufferings and struggles of the twentieth century," is the poetic counterpart to Miriam Davidson's prose memoir. It is based upon a large body of work associated with resistance to war and injustice by 144 poets around the world, many of whom endured "exile, state censorship, political persecution, house arrest, torture, imprisonment, military occupation, warfare, and assassination."[8] Writers of previous generations, of course, including several discussed in the previous chapter, issued similar complaints about this bloody century. Stanley Kunitz's "Night Letter" (1944) spoke of a general evil:

> I suffer the twentieth century
> The nerves of commerce wither in my arm;
> Violence shakes my dreams,[9]

and Muriel Rukeyser said that because "a lot of things have killed and mutilated people I love," she was willing to protest all of her life. . . . "I think Beethoven said, 'Everything I see is against my religion,' and I feel that way."[10]

For a younger generation, the suffering of this century has deepened in a peculiar way as "the normative promises of the nation-state have failed," Forche said, so that individual citizens do not enjoy, in some basic sense, "the solidarity that the concept of the nation is supposed to provide."[11] Perhaps this is why the plea for a new sense of communality informs much of the recent literature associated with nonviolence. Before and since the publication of *Against Forgetting,* poetry collections by several American writers—including Forche herself, June Jordan, Mark Pawlak, and David Williams—focus on this theme, as a new generation of men and women sing their songs about dark times, as Bertolt Brecht promised they would.

Such works speak, as with the memoir, *Convictions of the Heart,* about new alliances between landless peasants facing death in their home countries, from military or paramilitary groups armed and financed by the U.S. government, and ordinary citizens in the United States risking jail in order to protect refugees when they arrive here for political asylum. A central characteristic, if not theme, is a kind of redefinition of community, a major concern of the nonviolent tradition throughout its history.

June Jordan, in a preface to *Living Room,* poems written during the first Reagan administration, spoke very directly about this new understanding of community. Knowing "that there is no one anywhere suffering from injustice who is outside the moral measurement of my own life, whether in Detroit, Beirut, Teotecacinte, or Soweto," she committed herself, as an artist, to "work as hard as I can to help preserve and create living room on this only earth of ours."[12] It is an ambitious project, one that has previously overwhelmed writers, even with the best intentions. Experienced readers are understandably skeptical about "global" projects of any kind, including the language associated with them. One can point, nonetheless, to recent literature that successfully fulfills that expectation, addressing questions about how to live fully and responsibly in a community that reaches beyond national borders.

Among those determined to maintain this link with "the victims," Carolyn Forche has made a particular contribution, through the anthology already mentioned and in her own poetry, including the following bit of advice from "Ourselves or Nothing":

> Go after that which is lost
> and all the mass graves of the century's dead
> will open into your early working hours:[13]

In bringing together experience and artists from diverse cultures focusing on this theme, Forche maintains the nonviolent tradition's preoccupation with courage and faith: "The resistance to terror is what makes the world habitable," she said in the preface to *Against Forgetting,* "the protest against violence will not be forgotten and this insistent memory renders life possible in communal situations."

The danger of forgetting, of losing whole clusters of people and events, haunts the work of other recent American writers as well, who emphasize the writer's effort to recover voices that have been silenced and to make room for unrepresented people. In *Traveling Mercies: Poems* (1993), David Williams, a Lebanese American, for example, writes about so many "lost, unnamed, / unsanctified by memory," and about his poems as, among other things, a means of reclaiming them:

> The people I come from were thrown away
> as if they were nothing, whatever they might have
> said become stone, beyond human patience,
> except for the songs.

In several poems, Williams recognizes the similarity between his own background and that of nameless Central American refugees whom he has tried to assist, to "reclaim," through the Sanctuary movement.

> But what is all their daily
> breath against all the ardent, cunning
> justifications for murder?

In answering this question, Williams focuses on his—that is, the writer's —responsibility to resist the violence of history, by learning their songs and telling their stories: "The stunned drone of grief . . . the fierce tender undertone that bears up the world."[14]

For this essential work to continue, however, writers must resist the silence imposed on victims past and present. Otherwise literature—poetry, fiction, and memoir—will become simply another prop for the violence of the status quo. In this elemental struggle, there may be no middle ground, according to Czeslaw Milosz:

> What is poetry which does not save
> Nations or people?
> A connivance with official lies,
> A song of drunkards
>   whose throats will be cut in a moment, . . .[15]

In a culture that perpetuates itself by ignoring powerful forces misshaping our lives and our history and encourages us to cooperate with those forces, it is obviously not easy to hold on, to remain faithful, to a disquieting and radical perspective.

In "Entering History," a poem on a similar theme published shortly before his death, William Stafford described, for example, how money is seized against our will to perpetuate the violence that many of us abhor (a theme in Thoreau's "Civil Disobedience," mentioned earlier):

> You didn't want to
> give it but they took your money
> for those lethal tanks and the bombs.
> . . . Which bombs did you buy
> for the death rain that fell? Which year's
> taxes put that fire to the town
> where the screaming began?[16]

Wendell Berry has also described the cumulative effect of indifference to corporate violence, killing "by design, deliberately, without wrath." Are we likely to resort to tax resistance, as Thoreau and Ginsberg did, in addressing questions similar to those posed by Stafford? And how long can we retain Berry's humane perspective in "The Morning's News" (see above) when the media and other voices hammer away: "If it isn't entertaining, toss it out; if it challenges the perpetual present, forget it; and if you can't 'pretty it up,' demolish it"? Because values and activities associated with nonviolence do not quite "fit" theme parks or Disney worlds or "reconstructed" villages, will the tradition disappear completely?

"Only the truth will make us free. The whole truth, which is always awful."[17] And the surer our memory, in this violent century, the more pain we must integrate into our lives, associations, and institutions. Is that our surest guarantee against forgetting? And will American writers continue to assume that essential responsibility?

Without presuming to answer such questions, one might suggest, by way of conclusion, how the nonviolent tradition speaks to these questions, on the basis of the past initiatives and in light of recent circumstance.

As the previous chapters indicate, an extensive body of writings reflects numerous individual and communal efforts for nonviolent social change since at least the early European settlements. Even in the midst of expanding empire—from the first major war, 1846–48, to the present—poems, stories, essays, songs, and memoirs written by artists in the United States indicate a familiarity with philosophies and strategies of nonviolence.

It is a "tradition": a mode of thought, language, and behavior accessible in written documents and other artifacts, some of which represent a high degree of artistic achievement. It is a coherent body of ideas and images—a rhetoric—reflecting people's belief that the end (peace) is the sum total of the means (resisting injustice and resolving conflict) used to achieve it. As a tradition, nonviolence offers insights into how individuals and communities have achieved social change without violence to persons and perhaps into how we might work toward similar goals in the future.

In a culture as dynamic—and forgetful—as ours, where "nobody remembers anything past last Tuesday," as Gore Vidal has said, the history of and serious research on nonviolence have tended to move in circular rather than linear fashion. Some generations appear to have learned little from the ones that went before about the power of nonviolence and the skills essential to conducting campaigns for social change: vigils, marches, boycotts, strikes, sit-downs, mediation. Only occasionally, most notably in labor and civil rights movements, have activists and researchers set long-range goals and then chosen strategies for realizing them.

Most Americans grow up "illiterate" regarding nonviolent conflict resolution and active peacemaking. Most of us are all but helpless in dealing with conflicts in families, schools, neighborhoods, or among governments, and regard "the cult of violence . . . as if fists, guns, armies and nukes were sacred liturgies of a peace creed."[18] As a country with a sophisticated tradition of nonviolence, the United States lags behind other countries (Norway, Sweden, the Netherlands) in exploiting this element of its history. While other important achievements in American culture—public education, the distribution of goods and services, the orderly transfer of power within institutions—pass from one generation to the next, refined by each, nonviolence has to be relearned, almost from scratch.

Until now, study and research on nonviolence have enjoyed little institutional support from government, the university, or the church in the United States. "Teaching nonviolence" has been left to a handful of groups with limited personnel and financial support, such as the American Friends Service Committee, the Fellowship of Reconciliation, the War Resisters League, and the Catholic Worker movement. As of 1995, only one college in the United States (Colorado College) offers even a minor degree in nonviolence.

Reclaiming a place in the history of American culture, the nonviolent tradition has, since about 1960, won a minor victory, nonetheless, over formidable critical and academic opposition. Although military campaigns and military heroes and heroines still dominate social history, the great apostles of nonviolence gradually make their way into books, films, museums, and courses of study. Not surprisingly, the civil rights movement—Bayard Rustin, Glenn Smiley, Martin Luther King Jr., James Farmer, Barbara Deming, Vincent Harding—which revived interest in African American history and literature, reawakened interest in the oral and written literature of nonviolence along with them. At about the same time, academic disciplines associated with peace and global studies, even those confined to "the Western tradition," began to recognize roots, long-hidden, of a nonviolent past.

Religious institutions, including those grounded in beliefs professing "peace," still give lip service to nonviolence in official teaching. Although heroic in "reactive" relief efforts among victims throughout the world, these institutions are seldom "proactive" in addressing structural causes. Dom Helder Camara, the retired archbishop of Recife, Brazil, described the situation by saying: "If I feed the poor, I'm called a saint; if I address the causes of their hunger, I am called a communist."

Within Roman Catholicism, for example, the largest and wealthiest of the Christian denominations, the tradition of nonviolence received no official recognition until *The Challenge of Peace: God's Promise and Our Response* (1983). There, the American bishops recommended that Catholic colleges and universities become research centers for exploring nonviolent philosophy and strategy; a decade later, few academic institutions have responded. As with most colleges and universities, including others with religious affiliations, they seldom address what Howard Zinn has called "the monumental moral and tactical challenge of our time," that is, the effort to achieve justice without massive violence. And the elite empire schools—rich, powerful corporations—manage or cater to the military-industrial complex.

At a time when the distance between rich and poor steadily increases, with this country and its people armed to the teeth, the search for nonviolent means of resisting injustice and resolving conflict becomes ever more demanding and risky. Because violent means promise, though seldom provide, speedy results, those in power try to sell the public on the possibility of "surgical strikes" and similar kinds of military intervention. Not surprisingly, these quick solutions often lead to prolonged civil war, as the armaments disperse and multiply among the parties in conflict. In the end, antagonists return to long-delayed efforts to rebuild their societies: feeding the hungry, housing the homeless, resettling refugees, healing the wounded, building a civic culture.

These latter works of justice are obviously at the center of active peacemaking, and people who have done that work throughout American history have persistently dramatized the need for social change. During times of turmoil, as one might expect, the debate about how to guarantee "life, liberty, and the pursuit of happiness" has been especially lively: in decades just before the Revolutionary and Civil wars, in periods of industrial growth in the late nineteenth century and of waves of immigration in the early twentieth century, during the "militant thirties" and the civil rights and antiwar movements of the 1960s.

In each period, discussions about strategy—whether to rely on violence or nonviolence—took place at every level, from the family to the most encompassing national institutions. Which should it be: tactics associated with police and guns or social programs and direct action carried out by ordinary citizens or both? Along the way, Americans tolerated, justified, or endorsed policies that they regarded as consistent with democratic reform and human rights, but which, in many cases, further centralized power, marginalized the poor, and benefited not the many but the few. Although pretending to be untouched and unchanged by these imperial policies, this nation has come to represent, for a good portion of the world, the very callousness and brutality from which it said initially it would rescue humankind.

Recent examples of the United States choosing violence as a first, rather than a last, resort are numerous: in Korea (1951–53), the Dominican Republic (1965), Lebanon (1958 and 1983), Vietnam (1962–75), Grenada (1983), Libya (1986), Panama (1989), the Persian Gulf (1991)—all with disastrous results. President William Clinton's cruise missiling of Iraqi headquarters in Baghdad (and a scattering of nearby residences) in the summer of 1993 represented a continuation of such policies. Though declared a "success" by the government, this "secretly planned, unilateral act of violence . . . missed all the miscreants, made martyrs out of a couple of dozen Iraqi civilians, infuriated the Muslim world because of the feckless U.S. record in Bosnia and set back the development of a collective approach to world order," as Robert Ryan said.[19] Various alternatives to "violence as a first resort" might have failed as well, of course. But unfamiliar with or hostile to a language of nonviolence, the leadership and the general public seemed unlikely to choose a less belligerent policy.

Because a rhetoric of violence has dominated much of American life and culture since the Second World War, the means of social change (the threat of killing) shaped, perhaps determined, the end (violence): increased arms sales at home and abroad; escalated domestic violence; a larger prison population than any among industrialized nations in the world; and squandered human and natural resources, with universities undermined by programs related to chemical, biological, and nuclear weapons and "globalization from above."

Johan Galtung has argued that any vision of a civil society (or a world order) must take into account four types of power: military, economic, cultural, and political.[20] The fact that literary artifacts dramatize—through imagery, argument, and sound—the complex workings of power, from family and interpersonal relationships to international mediation, is a compelling reason for attending to them in our attempts to understand a violent world and to envision a peaceful one.

In recent American literature, a number of writers have been persistent, perceptive, and artful in describing this state of affairs and the attendant decline in public discourse. In a more compassionate mood than usual, Gore Vidal once identified the problem in this way:

> Most Americans lack the words, the concepts that might help them figure out what has happened; and it is hardly their fault. Simple falsities have been drummed into their heads from birth (socialism = Sweden = suicide) so that they will not rebel, not demand what is being withheld them. . . . social justice.[21]

Amid all this warmaking, individuals and small communities persist, nonetheless, in addressing the condition that Vidal so accurately describes and in upholding values in conflict with the dominant culture at considerable personal sacrifice and political risk. In the closing years of this century, as previously, one happens upon efforts of this kind when he or she least expects them: Committee Opposed to Militarism and the Draft, San Diego; Pikes Peak Coalition for Justice and Peace, Colorado Springs; St. Martin's Table, Minneapolis; Jonah House, Baltimore; Martin Luther King Center for the Study of Nonviolence, Los Angeles; and Catholic Worker farms and Houses of Hospitality in places you never heard of.

One of the best safeguards "against forgetting," in a manner similar to that of Miriam Davidson and Carolyn Forche, is building and supporting communities that keep the history of nonviolence alive from day to day. Through them, as through the expository and imaginative writings about them, one comes to appreciate the tradition. One rediscovers attitudes entertained and paths charted by people at crucial times in our history— paths acknowledged, but often rejected by those pursuing the course of empire: economic domination, territorial expansion, manifest destiny, mutual assured destruction.

The more we know about the nonviolent experiment and its legacy, the better we will understand the people and communities that continue, against enormous odds, to live similar values. They provide an opportunity to wonder "what might have been," if more Americans—labor leaders and academics, for example—had abided by Eugene Victor Debs's pledge "to rise with the people instead of from them."

Speaking of America's revolutionary origins, Page Smith once recommended our drawing on that history, "if we are to heal the division of our nation and have a reasonable prospect of creating a human future, not only for Americans, but for all the people who inhabit this greatly diminished globe."[22] A significant aspect of those "radical" origins was the effort to establish a peaceable kingdom and to sustain a community of people who simply refused to kill.

Anyone concerned about the future of human rights, ecology, and peace has much to learn from such communities and literature associated with them. They offer choices in our attempts to define ourselves and to interact with others in ways that preclude dominance and exploitation and waste.

Understanding how and why nonviolence "works" or does not "work" in a particular context, however, will require much more systematic study and information from a variety of sources than is already available. Just as most Americans are ignorant of their tradition of nonviolence, so French, Chinese, Russian, South African, and Indian activists and researchers are similarly handicapped. For that reason, research and detailed studies about how a particular culture informs, supports, or resists nonviolence will be important to our understanding of the past and to nonviolent activists of the present.

Thus far, the possibility of our living as responsible "citizens of the world," as nonviolent activists and writers have envisioned, is limited. Globalization—what might be a process of integration and cooperation —has been principally a process of top-down management. Six or eight powerful nations or, in some cases, multinational corporations dominate the world militarily, economically, and—when the United Nations cooperates with them—diplomatically. Without significant changes, this pattern (whether one calls it the old or the new world order) will continue.

If Richard Falk and other peace researchers are correct, "globalization-from-above" will follow the pattern that defines the economic life of the United States since World War II—a struggle between a management/government elite and everyone else. The rich will get richer, the poor, poorer, with economic devastation among poor nations, for example, and increasing numbers of unemployed, homeless, and impoverished in the industrial nations—in a word, disaster. The alternative, "globalization-from-below," a good synonym for nonviolence, offers "a crucible for creativity and resistance," with potentialities for engagement in all arenas of activity—local and global, private and public.[23]

In attempting to build a "new world order" with just working conditions, a healthy environment, and women's rights, ordinary people—that is, 90 percent of the population—may rediscover what advocates of nonviolence in the United States have maintained, that their allegiance belongs not to one nation, one class, one sex, but to the whole human family. In embracing Thomas Paine's self-definition as "citizen of the world," they may find other values of the nonviolent tradition equally relevant, including Eugene Victor Debs's: "While there is a lower class, I am in it; while there is a criminal element, I am of it; while there is a soul in prison, I am not free."

What aspects of the American tradition of nonviolence might contribute to this global process? Or are the laws and philosophical, artistic, and political traditions of this country so peculiar that they will serve only campaigns directed at American policies and institutions?

Nonviolence, like other means of political change, is culture-conscious, even culture-bound. For this reason, one must, in any campaign, think carefully about goals and strategies, ways of encouraging potential antagonists to identify with a cause and to join hands against the forces that oppress people or threaten a long and happy life. Chinese students during the 1989 uprising, for example, like U.S. draft resisters during the Vietnam War, were wise to associate their cause with symbols native to their country, rather than with "outside agitators." One can learn from foreign heroes and heroines, no doubt—as Danish war resisters learned from Henry David Thoreau and civil rights activists learned from Gandhi; but in speaking truth to power, people must choose signs and sayings out of their own history and culture, rather than adopt those belonging to completely different circumstances and traditions.

At the same time, one learns a great deal by comparing what worked in one setting with what did or did not work in another. And understanding the nonviolent tradition in the United States offers valuable insight into how revolutions win "the hearts and minds of the people" (John Adams's words) without resorting to violent means of resisting injustice and domination.

An important prerequisite for making peace, Kenneth Boulding said, is the construction of a social theory—an "intellectual chassis"—that is adequate "to support the powerful moral engine that drives it."[24] Close attention to the literature of the nonviolent tradition described in this book is central to that task: not only political and philosophical writings and psychological and sociological tracts but also poems, essays, stories, and other significant cultural artifacts.

In recent U.S. history, the civil rights movement, followed by the antiwar and Sanctuary movements, made visible a tradition associated with worker's and women's rights and anti-imperialist campaigns of the past three centuries. And its literature deepened a cultural commitment to resisting subjugation and violence and to extending, little by little, the beloved community.

Notes
Bibliographical Essay
Index

Notes

Reclaiming a Tradition

1. Quoted in Peter Mayer, ed. *The Pacifist Conscience* (Chicago: Henry Regnery, 1967), 123.

2. Howard Zinn, "A Century of Violence and Resistance," *Peacework* 232 (July/Aug. 1993): 3.

3. John Beecher, *Collected Poems, 1924–1974* (New York: Macmillan, 1974), 230–31.

4. Quoted in Gay Wilson Allen, *The New Walt Whitman Handbook* (New York: New York Univ. Press, 1986), 117.

5. Robert Bly, *The Light Around the Body* (New York: Harper and Row, 1967), 14.

6. *Agrarian Justice*, in *Thomas Paine: Representative Selections, With Introduction, Bibliography, and Notes,* rev. ed, ed. by Harry Hayden Clark (New York: Hill and Wang, 1961), 347.

7. James M. Washington, ed. *A Testament of Hope: The Essential Writings of Martin Luther King, Jr.* (New York: Harper and Row, 1986), 233.

8. Thomas Merton, ed. *Gandhi on Nonviolence: Selected Texts from Mohandas K. Gandhi's "Nonviolence in Peace and War"* (New York: New Directions, 1965), 37.

9. Dorothy Day, *On Pilgrimage: The Sixties* (New York: Curtis, 1972), 19.

10. E. J. Hobsbawm, *Revolutionaries: Contemporary Essays* (New York: New American, 1975), 209.

11. Sheldon Wolin, "Violence and the Western Political Tradition," *American Journal of Orthopsychiatry* 33 (Jan. 1963): 15–28.

12. Pauline Maier, *From Resistance to Revolution: Colonial Radicals and the Development of American Opposition to Britain, 1765–1776* (New York: Knopf, 1974), xii.

13. William Meredith, *Partial Accounts: New and Selected Poems* (New York: Knopf, 1987), 175.

14. Burritt, in Staughton Lynd, ed. *Nonviolence in America: A Documentary History* (Indianapolis: Bobbs Merrill, 1966), 97–98.

15. Merle Curti, *Peace or War: The American Struggle 1636–1936* (New York: Norton, 1936), 14.

16. Mulford Sibley, *The Political Theories of Modern Pacifism* (Philadelphia: The Peace Research Bureau, 1970), 67.

17. Brayton Shanley, "Pacifism and Intervention," *The Servant Song* 3, no. 1 (Summer 1993): 1.

18. Maier, 28.

19. Among many books emphasizing the transforming power of the struggle for independence, see Elisha P. Douglass, *Rebels and Democrats: The Struggle for Equal Political Rights and Majority Rule During the American Revolution* (1955; reprint, Chicago: Ivan R. Dee, 1989); and Gordon Wood, *The Radicalism of the American Revolution* (New York: Knopf, 1992).

20. Howard Zinn, *Disobedience and Democracy: Nine Fallacies on Law and Order* (New York: Vintage, 1968), 7.

21. J. Franklin Jameson, *The American Revolution Considered as a Social Movement* (Princeton: Princeton Univ. Press, 1926), 100.

1. The Peaceable Kingdom, 1607–1776

1. Quoted in Peter Brock, *Pacifism in the United States: From the Colonial Era to the First World War* (Princeton: Princeton Univ. Press, 1968), 218–19.

2. Charles M. Segal and David C. Stineback, *Puritans, Indians, and Manifest Destiny* (New York: Putnam's, 1977), 185.

3. "Germantown Friends' Protest Against Slavery," in Angie O'Gorman, ed. *The Universe Bends Toward Justice: A Reader on Christian Nonviolence in the U.S.* (Philadelphia: New Society, 1990), 21.

4. Brock, 83.

5. Ibid., 87.

6. John Woolman, *The Journal and Major Essays,* ed. Phillips P. Moulton (New York: Oxford Univ. Press, 1971), 127.

7. Brock, 51.

8. Woolman, 77.

9. Brock, 191.

10. Benezet, in Lynd, ed., 22–23.

11. Brock, 255.

12. Gary B. Nash, "Social Change and the Growth of Prerevolutionary Urban Radicalism," in *The American Revolution,* ed. Alfred Young (DeKalb: Northern Illinois Univ. Press, 1976), 27.

13. Maier, xv.

14. Quoted in Staughton Lynd, *Intellectual Origins of American Radicalism* (New York: Random House, 1968), 135.

15. *Prospects on the Rubicon,* in Philip S. Foner, ed. *The Complete Writings of Thomas Paine,* vol. 2 (New York: Citadel, 1945), 624.

16. Quoted in David Freeman Hawke, *Paine* (New York: Harper and Row, 1974), 277.

17. Thomas Paine, "Dissertation on First Principles of Government," *Common Sense and Other Political Writings,* ed. Nelson F. Adkins (Indianapolis: Bobbs Merrill, 1973), 174.

18. *Thomas Paine: Representative Selections,* 347.

19. Jefferson's "little book" is discussed in Stephen Mitchell, *The Gospel According to Jesus: A New Translation and Guide To His Essential Teachings for Believers and Unbelievers* (New York: HarperCollins, 1991), 3–10.

20. Lynd, *Intellectual Origins,* 4.

2. Passive Resistance, 1776–1865

1. *Thomas Paine: Representative Selections,* 57.

2. Maier, 3.

3. Brock, 366.

4. Ibid., 529.

5. Martin Henry Blatt, *Free Love & Anarchism: The Biography of Ezra Heywood* (Urbana: Univ. of Illinois Press, 1989), 15.

6. Brock, 382.

7. Lynd, 27.

8. Emerson, in Mayer, 122.

9. Brock, 543.

10. Adin Ballou, "Preface," *Christian Non-Resistance, in All Its Important Bearings, Illustrated and Defended* (Philadelphia: J. Miller M'Kim, 1846), 108–9.

11. Ibid., 109

12. Brock, 624.

13. Ballou, 108–9.

14. Merle Eugene Curti, ed. *The Learned Blacksmith: The Letters and Journals of Elihu Burritt* and *A Congress of Nations* (1937; reprint, New York: Garland, 1972).

15. Lynd, ed., 106.

16. Dorothy Sterling, *Ahead of Her Time: Abby Kelley and the Politics of Antislavery* (New York: Norton, 1991), 236–37.

17. Sterling, 387.

18. Sacvan Bercovitch, *The Rites of Assent: Transformations in the Symbolic Construction of America* (New York: Routledge, 1993), 226.

19. James Mellow, *Nathaniel Hawthorne in His Times* (Boston: Houghton Mifflin, 1980).

3. Labor Agitation and Religious Dissent, 1865–1914

1. "There is Power in the Union," in Leon Litwack, *The American Labor Movement* (New York: Simon and Schuster, 1962), 46–47.

2. Richard Hofstadter, "Introduction," *The Progressive Movement, 1900–1915* (Englewood Cliffs, N.J.: Prentice-Hall, 1963), 1.

3. Blatt, 4.

4. Ibid., 60.

5. Leo Tolstoy, *Writings on Civil Disobedience and Nonviolence* (Philadelphia: New Society, 1987), 413.

6. Charles DeBenedetti, *The Peace Reform in American History* (Bloomington: Indiana Univ. Press, 1980), 77.

7. Jim Zwick, ed. *Mark Twain's Weapons of Satire: Anti-imperialist Writings on the Philippine-American War* (Syracuse: Syracuse Univ. Press, 1992), xviii.

8. Zwick, xviii.

9. DeBenedetti, 76.

10. Zwick, 40.

11. Bourne to Van Wyck Brooks in *The World of Randolph Bourne: An Anthology of Essays and Letters,* ed. Lillian Schlissel (New York: Dutton, 1965), 316.

12. Bourne, 243.

13. "Address on the Philippine Question" in *William James: Writings 1902–1910* (New York: Library of America, 1987), 1131.

14. Quoted in Robert A. Rosenstone, *Romantic Revolutionary: A Biography of John Reed* (New York: Random House, 1975), 327.

15. Nick Salvatore, *Eugene V. Debs: Citizen and Socialist* (Urbana: Univ. of Illinois Press, 1982), 229–30.

16. Philip S. Foner, *The Case of Joe Hill* (New York: International, 1965), 11.

17. *Bill Haywood's Book: The Autobiography of William D. Haywood* (New York: International, 1929), 297.

18. Mary Fell, *The Persistence of Memory: Poems* (New York: Random House, 1984), 4.

19. Quoted in Philip S. Foner, *Women and the American Labor Movement: From the First Trade Unions to the Present* (New York: Free, 1982), 169.

20. Quoted in Henry F. May, *The End of American Innocence: A Study of the First Years of Our Own Time, 1912–1917* (New York: Knopf, 1959), 306.

21. Quoted in Rosenstone, 110.

22. *The Poems of Stanley Kunitz 1928–1978* (Boston: Little, Brown, 1979), 42.

23. Robert Ellsberg, ed. *By Little and By Little: The Selected Writings of Dorothy Day* (New York: Knopf, 1983), 146.

24. Elizabeth Gurley Flynn, *The Rebel Girl: An Autobiography—My First Life, 1906–1926* (New York: International, 1973).

25. Flynn, 294.

4. Draft Resistance and the Labor Movement, 1914–1940

1. Thomas McGrath, *Selected Poems 1938–1988,* ed. Sam Hammill (Port Townsend, Wash.: Copper Canyon, 1989), 114.

2. Salvatore, 288.

3. Bourne, 149.

4. Ibid., 78.

5. Ibid., 129.

6. Sudarshan Kapur, *Raising Up a Prophet: The African-American Encounter with Gandhi* (Boston: Beacon, 1992), 22–23.

7. Kapur, 90.

8. Quoted in Mel Piehl, *Breaking Bread: The Catholic Worker and the Origin of Catholic Radicalism in America* (Philadelphia: Temple Univ. Press, 1982), 66.

9. Dorothy Day, "Foreword to the First Edition," *The Book of Ammon,* 5th printing (n.p., 1970), 4th paragraph.

10. Hennacy, 26.

11. Ibid., 109.

12. Ibid., 136.

13. Lawrence S. Wittner, *Rebels Against War: The American Peace Movement, 1933–1983* (Philadelphia: Temple Univ. Press, 1984), 9.

14. Daniel Aaron, *Writers on the Left: Episodes in American Literary Communism* (1961; reprint, New York: Hippocrene Books, 1974).

15. Rukeyser, *The Collected Poems* (New York: McGraw-Hill, 1978), 84.

16. Quoted in Herbert Harris, "Sit-Down at General Motors," *The Thirties: A Time to Remember,* ed. Don Congdon (New York: Simon and Schuster, 1962), 493.

17. Meridel LeSueur, *Salute to Spring* (New York: International, 1977), 9.

18. "Homage to Thomas McGrath," in E. P. Thompson, *The Heavy Dancers* (London: Merlin, 1985), 284.

19. Thomas McGrath, *Letter to an Imaginary Friend, Parts I & II* (Chicago: Swallow, 1962, 1970), 52–54.

5. Conscientious Objection and Civil Rights, 1940–1965

1. Vincent Harding, "The Freedom Movement and the Rise of Nationalism," in *America's Black Past: A Reader in Afro-American History,* ed. Eric Foner (New York: Harper and Row, 1970), 465.

2. Gordon C. Zahn, *Another Part of the War: The Camp Simon Story* (Amherst: Univ. of Massachusetts Press, 1979), v–vi.

3. Jim Bristol, "Conscription, Conscience and Resistance," *Friends Journal* 38, no. 1 (1992): 20.

4. Robert Ludlow, quoted in Zahn, 240.

5. Howard Schoenfeld, "The Danbury Story," in Mayer, 344.

6. Zahn, 6.

7. Kunitz, *Poems,* 151–52.

8. Ibid., 49–51.

9. Stanley Kunitz, *A Kind of Order, A Kind of Folly: Essays and Interviews* (Boston: Little, Brown, 1975), 54.

10. Kunitz, *Poems,* 93.

11. Robert Lowell, *Selected Poems* (New York: Farrar, Straus & Giroux, 1976), 91–92.

12. Ian Hamilton, *Robert Lowell: A Biography* (New York: Random House, 1982), 91.

13. Hamilton, 89.

14. Lowell, 175.

15. Philip Berrigan, *A Punishment for Peace* (New York: Harcourt, Brace and World, 1969), 120.

16. Karl Shapiro, *Collected Poems, 1940–1978* (New York: Random House, 1978), 96.

17. William Stafford, *Down in My Heart* (1947; reprint Swarthmore, Pa.: Bench, 1985), 8.

18. Stafford, 91–92.

19. Ibid., 46.

20. Zahn, viii.

21. Ibid., 82.

22. Thomas Merton, *The Nonviolent Alternative,* rev. ed., ed. Gordon C. Zahn (New York: Farrar, Straus & Giroux, 1980), 138.

23. Zahn, in Merton, xvii.

24. Reed Whittemore, "Reflections . . . ," in *Poet's Choice,* ed. Paul Engle and Joseph Langland (New York: Dial, 1962), 177–78.

25. Terrence Des Pres, *Praises & Dispraises: Poetry and Politics, the 20th Century* (New York: Penguin, 1989).

26. "Rules for Action," in Lynd, ed., 397.

27. Kapur, 138.

28. James Baldwin, *The Fire Next Time* (New York: Dell, 1971), 36–37.

29. Baldwin, 65.

30. Quoted in Marty Jezer, *Abbie Hoffman: American Rebel* (New Brunswick, N.J.: Rutgers Univ. Press, 1992), 115.

31. See Ann Charters, *The Portable Beat Reader* (New York: Penguin, 1992), 387–94.

32. Ed Sanders, "Introduction," *Tales of Beatnik Glory* (New York: Citadel, 1990), ii.

33. Ed Sanders in *An Anthology of New York Poets,* ed. Ron Padgett and David Shapiro (New York: Random House, 1970), 381.

34. "The Politics of Being Queer," in *Nature Heals: The Psychological Essays of Paul Goodman,* ed. Taylor Stoehr (New York: Free Life, 1977), 222.

35. Paul Goodman, "Preface," *The Society I Live in Is Mine* (New York: Horizon, 1962).

36. "A Causerie at the Military-Industrial," in *Drawing the Line: The Political Essays of Paul Goodman,* ed. Taylor Stoehr (New York: Free Life, 1977), 158.

6. The Peace Movement and War Resistance, Nuclear Disarmament, and Anti-imperialism, 1965–1990

1. Martin Jezer, "Sheep Meadow Graduation," in *We Won't Go: Personal Accounts of War Objectors,* ed. Alice Lynd (Boston: Beacon, 1968), 225.

2. James W. Tollefson, *The Strength Not to Fight: An Oral History of Conscientious Objectors of the Vietnam War* (Boston: Little, Brown, 1993), 6.

3. Walter Lowenfels, ed. *Where Is Vietnam? American Poets Respond: An Anthology of Contemporary Poems* (Garden City, N.Y.: Anchor, 1967), x.

4. Cynthia Kerman, "Kenneth Boulding and the Peace Research Movement," in *Peace Movements in America,* ed. Charles Chatfield (New York: Schocken, 1973), 134.

5. David Ignatow, *Tread the Dark: New Poems* (Boston: Little, Brown, 1978), 27.

6. Norman Mailer, *The Armies of the Night: History as a Novel, The Novel as History* (New York: New American Library, 1969), 287.

7. "Poetry: After Modernism," in *Harvard Guide to Contemporary American Writing,* ed. Daniel Hoffman (Cambridge, Mass.: Harvard Univ. Press, 1979), 460.

8. Robert Bly, *The Light Around the Body* (New York: Harper and Row, 1967), 30.

9. "Acceptance of the National Book Award for Poetry" and "War Is the Health of the State," in *Walking Swiftly: Writings & Images on the Occasion of Robert Bly's 65th Birthday,* ed. Thomas R. Smith (St. Paul: Abby, 1993), 268–74.

10. Michael True, ed. *Daniel Berrigan: Poetry, Drama, Prose* (Maryknoll, N.Y.: Orbis, 1988), 307.

11. True, 166.

12. Jack Cook, *Rags of Time: A Season in Prison* (Boston: Beacon, 1972).

13. Robert Mezey, "How Much Longer" and Marge Piercy, "The Peaceable Kingdom" and "Community," in *Campfires of the Resistance: Poetry from the Movement,* ed. Todd Gitlin (Indianapolis: Bobbs Merrill, 1971), 208–9, 215–17, and 232.

14. Wendell Berry, "The Morning's News," in *Collected Poems 1957–1982* (San Francisco: North Point, 1984), 109–10.

15. William Packard, ed. *The Craft of Poetry: Interviews from the "New York Quarterly"* (Garden City, N.Y.: Doubleday, 1974), 172.

16. Rukeyser, 450–51.

17. Ibid., 239.

18. Ibid., 413.

19. Ibid., 509–10.

20. Ibid., 491.

21. Ibid., 524.

22. William Stafford, "Meditation," in *Smoke's Way: Poems from Limited Editions, 1968–1981* (Port Townsend, Wash.: Grewolf, 1983), 83.

23. Stafford, "Smoke Signals," in *A Glass Face in the Rain: New Poems* (New York: Harper and Row, 1982), 11.

24. Stafford, "Globescope" in *A Scripture of Leaves* (Elgin, Ill.: Brethren, 1989).

25. Denise Levertov, *Poems 1960–1967* (New York: New Directions, 1983), 229–30.

26. Denise Levertov, *Breathing the Water* (New York: New Directions, 1987).

27. Bruce Weigl, *Song of Napalm: Poems* (New York: Atlantic Monthly, 1988).

28. Piercy, in Gitlin, 217–18.

29. Denise Levertov, *Candles in Babylon* (New York: New Directions, 1982), 86.

7. Against Forgetting: 1990 and After

1. Richard Falk, "The Making of Global Citizenship," in *Global Visions: Beyond the New World Order,* ed. Jeremy Brecher, John Brown Childs, and Jill Cutler (Boston: South End, 1993), 49.

2. Miriam Davidson, *Convictions of the Heart: Jim Corbett and the Sanctuary Movement* (Tucson: Univ. of Arizona Press, 1988), 154.

3. Davidson, 2.

4. Reports on recent initiatives in Eastern Europe appear in the quarterly publication *Nonviolent Sanctions: News from the Albert Einstein Institution.* The concept is discussed in Gene Sharp, *Civilian-Based Defense: A Post-Military Weapons System* (Princeton: Princeton Univ. Press, 1990).

5. Ursula K. Le Guin, *Dancing at the Edge of the World: Thoughts on Words, Women, Places* (New York: Grove, 1989), 148.

6. Davidson, 164.

7. Jim Corbett, quoted in Davidson, 158.

8. Carolyn Forche, ed. *Against Forgetting: Twentieth Century Poetry of Witness* (New York: Norton, 1993), 29.

9. Kunitz, *Poems,* 161.

10. Quoted in Packard, 172.

11. Forche, 45.

12. June Jordan, "Preface," *Living Room: New Poems* (New York: Thunder's Mouth, 1985).

13. Carolyn Forche, *The Country Between Us* (New York: Harper and Row, 1981), 55–56.

14. David Williams, *Traveling Mercies: Poems* (Cambridge, Mass.: Alice James, 1993), 41, 5.

15. Czeslaw Milosz, "Dedication," *The Collected Poems, 1931–1987* (New York: Ecco, 1988), 78.

16. William Stafford, "Entering History," *Nation* 256, no. 15 (1993): 534.

17. Friedrich Heer, quoted in Elizabeth Young-Bruehl, *Hannah Arendt: For Love of the World* (New Haven: Yale Univ. Press, 1982), 395.

18. Colman McCarthy, "Foreword," in O'Gorman, x. For a good, brief introduction to peace studies in the United States, see his "Peace Education: The Time Is Now," *Washington Post,* Dec. 29, 1992.

19. Robert Ryan, "Violence as a First Resort," *Boston Globe,* Saturday, July 10, 1993.

20. Johan Galtung, "Visioning a Peaceful World," in *Buddhism and Nonviolent Global Problem-Solving: Ulan Bator Explorations,* ed. Gleen D. Paige and Sarah Gilliatt (Honolulu: Center for Nonviolence Planning Project, Univ. of Hawaii, 1991).

21. Gore Vidal, *Matters of Fact and of Fiction (1973–1976)* (New York: Random House, 1974), 284.

22. Page Smith, *A People's History of the American Revolution: A New Age Now Begins,* vol. 1, (New York: McGraw Hill, 1976), 7.

23. Richard Falk, "Challenges of the Changing World Order," Plenary Address, International Peace Research Association, Fourteenth General Conference, Kyoto, Japan, July 27–31, 1992.

24. Quoted in Cynthia Kerman, "Kenneth Boulding and the Peace Research Movement," in *Peace Movements in America,* ed. Charles Chatfield (New York: Shocken, 1973), 133.

Bibliographical Essay

Book Title

"An energy field more intense than war" is a line from Denise Levertov, "Making Peace," *Breathing the Water* (New York: New Directions, 1987), 25.

Book Epigraphs

Quotes are from Virgil, *The Georgics,* I, 11. 50–53, trans. Smith Palmer Bowie (Chicago: Univ. of Chicago Press, 1966), 5; Muriel Rukeyser, *The Life of Poetry* (New York: William Morrow, 1974), inside front cover; and Toni Morrison, *Playing in the Dark: Whiteness and the Literary Imagination* (Cambridge, Mass.: Harvard Univ. Press, 1992), 4.

Preface

Kenneth Boulding distinguishes between stable and unstable, positive and negative peace in *Stable Peace* (Austin: Univ. of Texas Press, 1978).

Stafford's remark appears in his *You Must Revise Your Life* (Ann Arbor: Univ. of Michigan Press, 1986), 73.

Paul Goodman, often insightful on the psychology of nonviolence, discussed conflict in *People or Personnel: Decentralizing and the Mixed Systems* and *Like a Conquered Province: The Moral Ambiguity of America* (New York: Vintage, 1968).

Lynd's definition appears in his introduction to *Nonviolence in America: A Documentary History* (Indianapolis: Bobbs Merrill, 1965), xvii.

In the ongoing debate about whether human beings are innately violent, a booklet coauthored by social scientists throughout the world is indispensable: *The Seville Statement: Preparing the Ground for the Constructing of Peace,* ed. David Adams (Paris: UNESCO, 1991).

Daniel Berrigan's statement is from his *Portraits of Those I Love* (New York: Crossroads, 1984), 153.

Studies of American literature and culture that are relevant here include Richard Slotkin, *Regeneration Through Violence: The Mythology of the American Frontier, 1600–1860* (Middletown, Conn.: Wesleyan Univ. Press, 1973); Sacvan Bercovitch, *The American Jeremiad* (Madison: Univ. of Wisconsin Press, 1979), and *The Rites of Assent: Transformations in the Symbolic Construction of America* (New York: Routledge, 1993).

Martin Green's books that explore the relationship between literature and "empire" include *Dreams of Adventure, Deeds of Empire* (London: Routledge and Kegan Paul, 1980); *The Challenge of the Mahatmas: Dreams of Adventure, Deeds of Empire* (New York: Basic, 1983); and *Children of the Sun: A Narrative of "Decadence" in England after 1918* (New York: Basic, 1976).

Reclaiming a Tradition

Essential histories of nonviolence in the United States include Lynd, introduction to *Nonviolence in America;* Peter Brock, *Pacifism in the United States: From the Colonial Era to the First World War* (Princeton: Princeton Univ. Press, 1968) and *Twentieth-Century Pacifism* (New York: Van Nostrand, 1970); Charles Chatfield, *For Peace and Justice: Pacifism in America, 1914–1941* (Knoxville: Univ. of Tennessee Press, 1971); Lawrence S. Wittner, *Rebels Against War: The American Peace Movement 1933–1983* (Philadelphia: Temple Univ. Press, 1984); *Peace Movements in America,* ed. Charles Chatfield (New York: Schocken, 1973); Charles DeBenedetti, *The Peace Reform in American History* (Bloomington: Indiana Univ. Press, 1980); *The Power of the People: Active Nonviolence in the United States,* ed. Robert Cooney and Helen Michalowski (Philadelphia: New Society, 1987).

Valuable anthologies on nonviolence include the Lynd anthology; *The Pacifist Conscience,* ed. Peter Mayer (New York: Holt, Rinehart and Winston, 1966); *Protest: Pacifism and Politics: Some Passionate Views on War and Nonviolence,* ed. James Finn (New York: Random House, 1968); *Conscience in America: A Documentary History of Conscientious Objection in America, 1757–1967,* ed. Lillian Schlissel (New York: Dutton, 1968); *Blessed Are the Peacemakers,* ed. Allen and Linda Kirschner (New York: Popular Library, 1971); *Nonviolence in Theory and Practice,* ed. Robert L. Holmes (Belmont, Calif.: Wadsworth, 1990); *Nonviolence: A Reader in the Ethics of Action,* ed. Doris A. Hunger and Krishna Mallick (New Delhi: The Gandhi Peace Foundation, 1990); and *The Universe Bends Toward Justice: A Reader on Christian Nonviolence in the U.S.,* ed. Angie O'Gorman (Philadelphia: New Society, 1990).

War and Peace in Literature, ed. Lucy Dougall (Chicago: World Without War Council, 1982), lists and briefly describes literary works on the general theme.

Violence is carefully defined in Hannah Arendt, *Crises of the Republic: Lying in Politics, Civil Disobedience, On Violence, Thoughts on Politics and Revolution* (New York: Harcourt Brace Jovanovich, 1972); and Sheldon Wolin, "Violence and the Western Political Tradition," *American Journal of Orthopsychiatry* 33 (Jan. 1963): 15–28. *Nonviolence* is defined in Gene Sharp, *The Politics of Nonviolent Action* (Boston: Porter Sargent, 1973); Roger S. Powers, "Nonviolent Philosophy/Nonviolent Action: An Appeal for Conceptual Precision," *Nonviolent Sanctions* 5, no. 1 (Summer 1993), 4–6; and my "Nonviolence, Peace Movement, and Social Activism," *Peace and World Security Studies: A Curriculum Guide,* 6th ed., ed. Michael Klare (Boulder: Lynne Rienner, 1994), 396–405.

The contrasts between "peace reform" and "nonviolence" in the United States become obvious about 1914. Earlier valuable studies, in addition to those mentioned above, include Devere Allen, *The Fight for Peace* (New York: Macmillan, 1930), and Merle Curti, *Peace or War: The American Struggle, 1636–1936* (New York: Norton, 1936).

1. The Peaceable Kingdom, 1607–1776

Roger Williams's polemics and contributions are the subject of Edmund S. Morgan, *Roger Williams: The Church and the State* (New York: Harcourt, Brace and World, 1967). The early Quakers are discussed in Hugh Barbour and J. William Frost, *The Quakers* (New York: Greenwood, 1988); and D. Elton Trueblood, *The People Called Quakers* (New York: Harper and Row, 1966).

William Penn's vigorous, wide-ranging pamphlets are admirably edited and introduced by Mary Maples Dunn and Richard S. Dunn and others in *The Papers of William Penn,* 5 vols. (Philadelphia: Univ. of Pennsylvania Press, 1981), with additional commentary in Catherine Owens Peare, *William Penn: A Biography* (Ann Arbor: Univ. of Michigan Press, 1956). Jim Corbett discusses the covenant in chap. 10 of his *Goatwalking* (New York: Viking, 1991).

Staughton Lynd, *Intellectual Origins of American Radicalism* (New York: Random House, 1968) is an essential general survey, though the book's focus is nonviolence.

Strategies and tactics employed by nonviolent activists before the American Revolution are discussed in Gary N. Nash, "Social Change and the Growth of Prerevolutionary Urban Radicalism"; Marvin L. Michael Kay, "The North Carolina Regulation, 1766–1776"; and Dick Hoerder, "Boston Leaders and Boston Crowds, 1765–1776," in *The American Revolution: Explorations in the History of American Radicalism,* ed. Alfred Young (DeKalb: Northern Illinois Univ. Press, 1976). Also excellent are Pauline Maier, *From Resistance to Revolution: Colonial Radicals and the Development of American Opposition to Britain, 1760–1776* (New York: Knopf, 1972), and *The Old Revolutionaries: Political Lives in the Age of Samuel Adams* (New York: Random House, 1980).

David Freeman Hawke, *Paine* (New York: Harper and Row, 1974) is a good biography. Eric Foner's *Tom Paine and Revolutionary America* (New York: Oxford Univ. Press, 1976) studies the pamphleteer in his time. A standard, though incomplete, edition of Paine's writings is *The Complete Writings of Thomas Paine,* 2 vols., ed. Philip Foner (New York: Citadel, 1945). Paine had a genius for bringing together ideas and concepts that had circulated throughout the colonies since the beginning of the century; these ideas are discussed in Bernard Bailyn, *The Ideological Origins of the American Revolution* (Cambridge, Mass.: Harvard Univ. Press, 1967).

2. Passive Resistance, 1776–1865

Still valuable is Carl L. Becker, *The Declaration of Independence: A Study in the History of Political Ideas* (New York: Random House, 1942); see also Garry Wills, *Inventing America: Jefferson's Declaration of Independence* (New York: Random House, 1979). Emory Elliot, *Revolutionary Writers: Literature and Authority in the New Republic, 1725–1810* (New York: Oxford Univ. Press, 1982) documents the dissatisfaction that poets and novelists felt toward the new republic almost from the moment it was formed. A counterculture-in-the-making related to nonviolence is evident in the writings of Paine, Benjamin Rush, and in poems, novels, and essays by less activist artists and intellectuals.

Important studies of the abolitionists include Aileen S. Kraditor, *Means and Ends in American Abolitionism: Garrison and His Critics in Strategy and Tactics, 1834–1850* (New York: Pantheon, 1969). The relationship between the abolitionist and women's movements is a theme in Eleanor Flexner, *Century of Struggle: The Woman's Rights Movement in the United States* (New York: Atheneum, 1974). Garrison's influence is discussed in *Lucretia Mott: Her Complete Speeches and Sermons,* ed. Dana Greene (New York: Edwin Mellen, 1980); in Dorothy Sterling, *Ahead of Her Time: Abby Kelley and the Politics of Antislavery* (New York: Norton, 1991); and in Michael S. Kimmel's introduction to *Against the Tide: Pro-Feminist Men in the United States, 1776–1990—A Documentary History,* ed. Michael S. Kimmel and Thomas E. Mosmiller (Boston: Beacon, 1992).

In the pre-Civil War period, Nathaniel Hawthorne was as obsessed with violence in the new nation as were Garrison, Ballou, Burritt, and the Fosters; and so it is instructive to set Hawthorne's stories and novels beside essays by abolitionists and passive resisters. Also relevant are poems and essays by well-known literary figures, including John Greenleaf Whittier and James Russell Lowell. Valarie H. Ziegler, *The Advocates of Peace in Antebellum America* (Bloomington: Indiana Univ. Press, 1992) focuses on the American Peace Society in this period.

As Edward Needles Wright says, in *Conscientious Objectors in the Civil War* (Philadelphia: Univ. of Pennsylvania Press, 1931), C.O.s were referred to, at the time, as "non-resistants, non-combatants, those scrupulous against bearing arms." Significant documents on nonviolent resistance before and after the Civil War period appear in *Civil Disobedience in America: A Documentary History,* ed. David R. Weber (Ithaca: Cornell Univ. Press, 1978). *Dissent: Explorations in the History of American Radicalism,* ed. Alfred F. Young (DeKalb: Northern Illinois Univ. Press, 1968) includes useful essays on this period and after.

3. Labor Agitation and Religious Dissent, 1865–1914

Standard anthologies and histories often omit any mention of contributions by nonviolent activists or radical reformers to social movements. Among the thirty-six documents in *The Progressive Movement, 1900–1915,* ed. Richard Hofstadter (Englewood Cliffs, N.J: Prentice Hall, 1963), for example, there is nothing by Debs, Goldman, or Flynn. For the relationship between agitation for labor reform and nonviolence in the post-Civil War period, see Sidney Lens, *The Labor Wars: From the Molly Maguires to the Sit-Downs* (Garden City, N.Y.: Doubleday, 1973); Richard Boyer and Herbert Morais, *Labor's Untold Story* (New York: United Electrical R. and M., 1955); and Philip S. Foner, *Women and the American Labor Movement: From the First Trade Unions to the Present* (New York: Free, 1982). In addition to the works mentioned by Howells, the novels of Frank Norris, Jack London, Upton Sinclair, and Rebecca Harding Davis dramatize the labor struggles of the period 1890–1910. Leon Litwack, *The American Labor Movement* (New York: Simon and Schuster, 1962) provides an excellent sampling of labor songs, poems, and manifestos.

Leo Tolstoy's anti-imperial pamphlets and letters (some collected in *Writings on Civil Disobedience and Nonviolence* [Philadelphia: New Society, 1987]) were admired by Americans who knew little about his indebtedness to Garrison, Ballou, and Burritt.

Long before he published "The Moral Equivalent of War" (1910), William James was active in the New England Anti-imperialist League, as indicated in "Address on the Philippine Question," *William James: Writings 1902–1910* (New York: Library of America, 1987), though one would hardly know that from Gay Wilson Allen's *William James* (New York: Viking, 1967). Mark Twain's antiwar writings, long ignored, are collected in *Mark Twain's Weapons of Satire: Anti-imperialist Writings on the Philippine-American War,* ed. Jim Zwick. (Syracuse: Syracuse Univ. Press, 1992); this book, more than any other, helps to explain Twain's reputation among social critics, such as Van Wyck Brooks and Randolph Bourne, shortly after Twain's death.

Allen F. David, *American Heroine: The Life and Legend of Jane Addams* (New York: Oxford Univ. Press, 1973) provides insights into a complex and truly great figure.

An indispensable study of the relationship between art and social change before World War I, when young writers allied themselves with the Wobblies, socialists, and anarchists, is Henry F. May, *The End of American Innocence: A Study of the First Years of Our Own Time, 1912–1917* (New York: Knopf, 1959). Martin Green, *New York 1913: The Armory Show and the Paterson Strike Pageant* (New York: Scribner's, 1988), although it omits discussion of political repression during and just after the war that crushed the labor movement, is useful. The relationship between political and aesthetic values in early modernism is discussed in Edward Abrahams, *The Lyrical Left: Randolph Bourne, Alfred Stieglitz, and the Origins of Cultural Radicalism in America* (Charlottesville: Univ. of Virginia Press), 1986.

4. Draft Resistance and the Radical Decade, 1914–1940

Walter Bates Rideout, *The Radical Novel in the United States, 1900–1954: Some Interrelations of Literature and Society* (Cambridge, Mass.: Harvard Univ. Press, 1956) discusses literary works important to nonviolent activists. Other relevant literary and cultural histories are Richard H. Pells, *Radical Visions and American Dreams: Culture and Social Thought in the Depression Years* (New York:

Harper and Row, 1973), and Daniel Aaron, *Writers on the Left: Episodes in American Literary Communism* (New York: Hippocrene, 1974). Useful anthologies of fiction and poetry of the 1930s include *The American Writers and the Great Depression,* ed. Harvey Swados (Indianapolis: Bobbs Merrill, 1966), and *The Thirties: A Time to Remember,* ed. Don Congdon (New York: Simon and Schuster, 1962).

On the principal figures and literature of the Catholic Worker movement, see Mel Piehl, *Breaking Bread: The Catholic Worker and the Origins of Catholic Radicalism in America* (Philadelphia: Temple Univ. Press, 1982); William Miller, *A Harsh and Dreadful Love: Dorothy Day and the Catholic Worker Movement* (New York: Liveright, 1973), as well as the introduction to *Selected Writings of Dorothy Day,* ed. Robert Ellsberg (Maryknoll, N.Y.: Orbis, 1993).

Sudarshan Kapur, *Raising Up A Prophet: The African-American Encounter with Gandhi* (Boston: Beacon, 1992) discusses Gandhi's influence on African Americans resisting segregation in the United States, between 1920 and 1947. Related documents appear in *Black Protest Thought in the Twentieth Century,* 2d ed., ed. August Meier, Elliot Rudwick, and Francis L. Broderick (New York: Macmillan, 1971).

Meridel LeSueur's best writing appears in *Salute to Spring* (New York: International, 1977).

5. Conscientious Objection and Civil Rights, 1940–1965

Leonard S. Kenwothy, "The Impact of CPS," *Friends Journal* 3, no. 1 (Jan. 1992), 14–17, discusses the leadership roles assumed by C.O.s after the war; in the same issue, Jim Bristol, "Conscription, Conscience, and Resistance," 20–21, discusses the hard choices faced by religious pacifists who could not, in conscience, cooperate with the Selective Service in accepting C.O. status. A standard work is Mulford Sibley and P. E. Jacob, *Conscription of Conscience: The American State and the Conscientious Objector, 1940–1947* (Ithaca: Cornell Univ. Press, 1952). A brief portrait of Sibley appears in my *Justice Seekers, Peacemakers: 32 Portraits in Courage* (Mystic, Conn.: XXIII Publications, 1985).

Three excellent memoirs by pacifists are William Stafford, *Down in My Heart* (Swarthmore, Pa: Bench, 1985); Gordon Zahn, *Another Part of the War: The Camp Simon Story* (Amherst: Univ. of Massachusetts Press, 1979), both were conscientious objectors; and David Dellinger, *From Yale to Jail: The Life Story of a Moral Dissenter* (New York: Pantheon, 1993), a draft resister. Among the various editions of Zahn's influential book, see esp. *In Solitary Witness: The Life and Death of Franz Jagerstatter* (Boston: Beacon, 1969), with a preface by James Harney, a Boston-area priest who was jailed for burning draft records as a member of the Milwaukee 14. Francine du Plessix Gray, *Divine Disobedience: Profiles in Catholic Radicalism* (New York: Random House, 1970) discusses the "Catholic conspiracy against the war in Vietnam," as Zahn called it, and the increasing involvement of people from similar religious backgrounds.

Reed Whittemore's poem first appeared in *Sewanee Review* 64, no. 1 (Winter 1956). *Howl* appears in Allen Ginsberg, *Collected Poems 1947–1980* (New York:

Harper and Row, 1984). Ed Sanders's introduction to and stories in *Tales of Beatnik Glory* (New York: Citadel, 1990) indicate the contributions of writers to the antiwar movement, including the hilarious "folk ensemble of poets," the Fugs. Marty Jezer, *Abbie Hoffman: American Rebel* (New Brunswick, N.J.: Rutgers Univ. Press, 1992) is valuable on the New York scene.

The San Francisco Renaissance, like the early modernist movement, maintained important connections between art and radical politics, particularly pacifism, as noted in Lee Bartlett, *William Everson: The Life of Brother Antoninus* (New York: New Directions, 1988) and Linda Hamalian, *A Life of Kenneth Rexroth* (New York: Norton, 1991). Todd Gittlin's history of the decade, *The Sixties: Years of Hope, Days of Rage* (New York: Bantam, 1987), is complemented by *The Sixties Papers: Documents of a Rebellious Decade*, ed. Judith Clavir Albert and Stewart Edward Albert (New York: Praeger, 1984).

Relevant poems by Thomas McGrath appear in his *Letter to an Imaginary Friend, Parts I & II* (Chicago: Swallow, 1970) and *Selected Poems: 1938–1988* (Port Townsend, Wash.: Copper Canyon, 1988).

Taylor Branch, *Parting the Waters: America in the King Years 1954–63* (New York: Simon and Schuster, 1988) discusses the influence of Martin Luther King Jr. and the civil rights movement on the wider culture, as does the invaluable collection, *Voices of Freedom: An Oral History of the Civil Rights Movement from the 1950s through the 1980s,* ed. Henry Hampton and Steve Fayer, with Sarah Flynn (New York: Bantam, 1990). *A Testament of Hope: The Essential Writings of Martin Luther King, Jr.,* ed. James M. Washington (New York: Harper and Row, 1986) gathers most of King's writings. James Baldwin's *Notes of a Native Son* (1955) and *The Fire Next Time* (1963), collected in *The Price of the Ticket: Collected Nonfiction, 1948–1985* (New York: St. Martin's, 1985), include essays provoked by and important to the civil rights movement. Baldwin's frustrations with the Kennedy administration and the civil rights leadership are discussed in Branch (above) and James H. Cone, *Martin and Malcolm and America: A Dream or a Nightmare* (Maryknoll, N.Y.: Orbis, 1992), as is the relationship between (and conflict over) violent and nonviolent means in the black liberation movement. Other important literary works include the poems of Gwendolyn Brooks, especially *Selected Poems* (New York: Harper, 1963); Amiri Baraka [LeRoi Jones], especially *Black Magic: Collected Poetry 1961–1967* (Indianapolis: Bobbs Merrill, 1969); and Malcolm X, *The Autobiography of Malcolm X,* with Alex Haley (New York: Ballantine Books, 1973).

Barbara Deming, *Prison Notes* (Boston: Beacon 1966) is a useful memoir by a nonviolent strategist involved in the black and gay liberation movements, as well as the antiwar and antinuclear movements.

6. The Peace Movement and War Resistance, Nuclear Disarmament, and Anti-imperialism, 1965–1990

Writers' responses to the nuclear arms race, in addition to those previously cited, include *In a Dark Time: Images for Survival,* ed. Robert Jay Lifton and

Nicholas Humphrey (Cambridge, Mass.: Harvard Univ. Press, 1984); "Writers in the Nuclear Age," ed. Sydney Lea, *New England Review and Bread Loaf Quarterly* 5, no. 4 (Summer 1983); and *Nuke-Rebuke: Writers & Artists Against Nuclear Energy & Weapons,* ed. Morty Sklar (Iowa City, Iowa: The Spirit That Moves Us Press, 1984).

Charles DeBenedetti, *An American Ordeal: The Antiwar Movement of the Vietnam Era* (Syracuse: Syracuse Univ. Press, 1990), and Michael Ferber and Staughton Lynd, *The Resistance* (Boston: Beacon, 1971), survey the period 1965–75.

James F. Mersmann, *Out of the Vietnam Vortex: A Study of Poets and Poetry Against the War* (Lawrence: Univ. Press of Kansas, 1974) is the best book on poetry of that period. Theodore Roszak, *The Making of a Counter Culture: Reflections on the Technocratic Society and Its Youthful Opposition* (Garden City, N.Y.: Doubleday, 1968) has informative chapters on Goodman and Ginsberg. Richard King, *The Party of Eros: Radical Social Thought in the Realm of Freedom* (Chapel Hill: Univ. of North Carolina Press, 1972) is insightful on Goodman's writings.

The strength of grassroots movements for nonviolent social change since 1965 is evident in numerous organizations associated with the nuclear freeze, ecology, sanctuary, women's liberation, gays, and lesbians throughout the United States. Representative periodicals include *Active for Justice* (Colorado Springs: Pikes Peak Coalition for Justice and Peace); *Southern Exposure* (Durham, N.C.: Institute for Southern Studies); *Peacework* (Cambridge, Mass.: American Friends Service Committee). Also informative is *Peacework: 20 Years of Nonviolent Social Change,* ed. Pat Farren (Baltimore: Fortkamp, 1991).

A useful introductory text on peace studies and academic disciplines associated with it, such as conflict resolution and mediation, is David P. Barash, *Introduction to Peace Studies* (Belmont, Calif.: Wadsworth, 1991). *Peace Studies: The Hard Questions: Oxford Peace Lectures 1984–85,* ed. Elaine Kaye (London: Rex Collings, 1987) poses major questions addressed by the new discipline—or interdiscipline. *Peace and World Security Studies: A Curriculum Guide,* ed. Michael Klare, 6th ed. (Boulder, Colo.: Lynne Reiner, 1993) discusses the history of peace studies, with informative essays and syllabi.

Influential anthologies of poetry and statements about resistance to the war in Vietnam and after include *Poets Against the War in Vietnam,* ed. Robert Bly and David Ray (Madison, Minn.: Sixties, 1965); *Authors Take Sides on Vietnam: Two Questions on the War in Vietnam Answered by the Authors of Several Nations,* ed. Cecil Woolf and John Bagguley (New York: Simon and Schuster, 1967); *Women on War: Essential Voices for the Nuclear Age from a Brilliant International Assembly,* ed. Daniela Gioseffi (New York: Simon and Schuster, 1988).

Thomas Merton and Daniel Berrigan, as priests and poets, influenced nonviolent movements for social change after 1965. Gordon Zahn's excellent introduction to Thomas Merton, *The Nonviolent Alternative* (New York: Farrar, Straus, and Giroux, 1980) discusses Merton's essays on peace and social justice; my introduction to *Daniel Berrigan: Poetry, Drama, Prose* (Maryknoll, N.Y.: Orbis, 1988) emphasizes Berrigan's importance as writer, as well as a war resister. Among documents important to nonviolence, see also Philip Berrigan, *A Punishment for Peace* (New York: Harcourt, Brace and World, 1969), and *Swords into Plowshares: Nonviolent Direction Action*, ed. Arthur J. Laffin and Anne Montgomery (New York: Harper and Row, 1987).

Insightful commentaries on Rukeyser's writings appear in Louise Kertesz, *The Poetic Vision of Muriel Rukeyser* (Baton Rouge: Louisiana State Univ. Press, 1980), and on Levertov's writings in James E. B. Breslin, *From Modern to Contemporary American Poetry, 1945–1965* (Chicago: Univ. of Chicago Press, 1984), and *Denise Levertov: Selected Criticism*, ed. Albert Gelpi (Ann Arbor: Univ. of Michigan Press, 1993). Standard works are Muriel Rukeyser, *The Collected Poems* (New York: McGraw-Hill, 1978); Denise Levertov, *Poems, 1960–67* (New York: New Directions, 1983), as well as later collections of Levertov's poetry and *New and Selected Essays* (New York: New Directions, 1992).

Rukeyser and Levertov, Ginsberg, Bly, Gary Snyder, Adrienne Rich, June Jordan, Wendell Berry, Amiri Baraka (LeRoi Jones), Galway Kinnell, and others discuss the relationship between art and social change in *American Radical Thought: The Libertarian Tradition*, ed. Henry J. Silverman (Lexington, Mass.: Heath, 1970) and *Poetry and Politics: An Anthology of Essays*, ed. Richard Jones (New York: Quill, 1985). The later book includes Levertov's "On the Edge of Darkness: What Is Political Poetry," a relevant discussion of "commitment," about political urgency as "an almost hectic stimulus" for a poet living at the present time; Carolyn Forche's introduction to *Against Forgetting* (see below) is complementary and insightful on this theme.

Among Wendell Berry's several essay collections, see esp. *Standing By Words* (San Francisco: North Point, 1990).

7. Against Forgetting, 1990 and After

The influence of liberation theology in Latin America on movements for social change in the United States, including the Sanctuary movement, is discussed in Penny Lernoux, *The Cry of the People: United States Involvement in the Rise of Fascism, Torture, and Murder and the Persecution of the Catholic Church in Latin America* (New York: Doubleday, 1980) and *The People of God: The Struggle for World Catholicism* (New York: Viking, 1989). Philip Berryman, *The Religious Roots of Rebellion: Christians in Central American Revolutions* (Maryknoll, N.Y.: Orbis, 1984) discusses Ernesto Cardenal's indebtedness to Thomas Merton. An indispensable book on the Christian basis for nonviolence is Walter Wink, *Violence and Nonviolence in South Africa: Jesus' Third Way* (Philadelphia: New World, 1987).

The literary response in the United States to the struggle in Central America, in addition to Davidson's memoir and Forche's anthology, includes Joan Didion, *Salvador* (New York: Washington Square, 1983); Edward R. F. Sheehan, *Agony in the Garden: A Stranger in Central America* (Boston: Houghton Mifflin, 1988), a memoir about wars and upheaval, 1985–88; and his novel, *Innocent Darkness* (New York: Viking, 1993). Poetry collections reflecting similar themes and preoccupations are Mark Pawlak, *Special Handling: Newspaper Poems New and Selected* (Brooklyn: Hanging Loose, 1993), and David Williams, *Traveling Mercies: Poems* (Cambridge, Mass.: Alice James, 1993).

Useful attempts to understand a "new world order" include Howard Zinn, *Declarations of Independence* (New York: Harper and Row, 1990); essays by Richard Falk and others in *Global Visions: Beyond the New World Order,* ed. Jeremy Brecher, John Brown Childs, and Jill Cutler (Boston: South End, 1993); and Elise Boulding, *Building a Global Civic Culture: Education for an Interdependent World* (Syracuse: Syracuse Univ. Press, 1990).

The concept of power, so basic to all relationships and conflicts, and thus to nonviolence, is discussed in "Power," in *Encyclopedia of the Social Sciences;* Arendt's *Crises of the Republic* (mentioned above); and Kenneth Boulding, *Three Faces of Power* (Newbury Park, Calif.: Sage, 1988).

A useful guide to research on the "new" global order is *International Peace Research Newsletter,* published by the International Peace Research Association (IPRA), Antioch College, Yellow Springs, Ohio 45387; its North American affiliate is Consortium on Peace Research, Education, and Development (COPRED), George Mason Univ., Fairfax, Va. 22030–4444. Numerous initiatives for nonviolent social change in various countries of the world are noted in *Transforming Struggle: Strategy and the Global Experience of Nonviolent Direct Action* (Cambridge, Mass.: Harvard Univ. Center for International Affairs, 1992), and in publications of the Albert Einstein Institution, 50 Church Street, Cambridge, Mass. 02138. In them, activists and researchers often document what poets and novelists dramatize or describe about interdependency and community—traditional concerns of nonviolence.

Index

155

Syracuse Studies on Peace and Conflict Resolution
Harriet Hyman Alonso, Charles Chatfield, and Louis Kriesberg, *Series Editors*

A series devoted to readable books on the history of peace movements, the lives of peace advocates, and the search for ways to mitigate conflict, both domestic and international. At a time when profound and exciting political and social developments are happening around the world, this series seeks to stimulate a wider awareness and appreciation of the search for peaceful resolution to strife in all its forms and to promote linkages among theorists, practitioners, social scientists, and humanists engaged in this work throughout the world.

Other titles in the series include:

An American Ordeal: The Antiwar Movement of the Vietnam Era. Charles DeBenedetti; Charles Chatfield, assisting author

Building a Global Civic Culture: Education for an Interdependent World. Elise Boulding

Cooperative Security: Reducing Third World Wars. I. William Zartman and Victor A. Kremenyuk, eds.

The Eagle and the Dove: The American Peace Movement and United States Foreign Policy, 1900–1922. John Whiteclay Chambers II

From Warfare to Party Politics: The Critical Transition to Civilian Control. Ralph M. Goldman

Gandhi's Peace Army: The Shanti Sena and Unarmed Peacekeeping. Thomas Weber

Gender and the Israeli-Palestinian Conflict: The Politics of Women's Resistance. Simona Sharoni

The Genoa Conference: European Diplomacy, 1921–1922. Carole Fink

Give Peace a Chance: Exploring the Vietnam Antiwar Movement. Melvin Small and William D. Hoover, eds.

Human Rights in the West Bank and Gaza. Ilan Peleg

Intractable Conflicts and Their Transformation. Louis Kriesberg, Terrell A. Northrup, and Stuart J. Thorson, eds.

Israeli Pacifist: The Life of Joseph Abileah. Anthony Bing

Mark Twain's Weapons of Satire: Anti-imperialist Writings on the Philippine-American War. Mark Twain; Jim Zwick, ed.

One Woman's Passion for Peace and Freedom: The Life of Mildred Scott Olmsted. Margaret Hope Bacon

Organizing for Peace: Neutrality, the Test Ban, and the Freeze. Robert Kleidman

Peace as a Women's Issue: A History of the U.S. Movement for World Peace and Women's Rights. Harriet Hyman Alonso

Peace/Mir: An Anthology of Historic Alternatives to War. Charles Chatfield and Ruzanna Ilukhina, volume editors

Plowing My Own Furrow. Howard W. Moore

Polite Protesters: The American Peace Movement of the 1980s. John Lofland

Preparing for Peace: Conflict Transformation Across Cultures. John Paul Lederach

The Road to Greenham Common: Feminism and Anti-Militarism in Britain since 1820. Jill Liddington

Timing the De-escalation of International Conflicts. Louis Kriesberg and Stuart Thorson, eds.

Virginia Woolf and War: Fiction, Reality, and Myth. Mark Hussey, ed.

The Women and the Warriors: The U.S. Section of the Women's International League for Peace and Freedom, 1915–1946. Carrie Foster